MW01517855

RUN WITH A MIGHTY HEART

JENNIFER MORRISON

 FriesenPress

One Printers Way
Altona, MB R0G 0B0
Canada

www.friesenpress.com

ISBN
978-1-03-912838-5 (Hardcover)
978-1-03-912837-8 (Paperback)
978-1-03-912839-2 (eBook)

1. SPORTS & RECREATION, HORSE RACING

Distributed to the trade by The Ingram Book Company

For Shirley and Ewen, my Mom and Dad

Horses carry the wisdom of healing in their hearts and offer it to any human who possesses the humility to listen – Unknown

The first favourite was never heard of, the second favourite was never seen after the distance post, all the ten-to-oners were in the rear, and a dark horse, which had never been thought of...rushed past the grandstand to sweeping triumph. – Benjamin Disraeli, "The Young Duke"

Table of Contents

Foreword

ON MARCH 11, 2020, the domain of professional sports shut down as we faced the reality of a global pandemic, and a general sense of hopelessness overtook our world. It was no exception in Toronto, Ontario, as all major sports ground to a halt, and the script for the 2020 thoroughbred horse racing season was yet to be written.

The community at Toronto's Woodbine Racetrack is close-knit and passionate that shares a love of equine athletes. By bonding together, the community gave the sport every opportunity to proceed that spring by following health protocols and steadfastly preparing its athletes for a season that some doubted would happen. Each day brought new challenges and tensions with the threat of COVID-19, and we wondered whether life would ever return to normalcy. It was a desperate time, and we were all searching for a glimmer of joy.

Run With a Mighty Heart is an inspiring story about the journey of a one-eyed Thoroughbred racehorse who uplifted the spirits of a nation during the worst crisis of most of our lifetimes. With patience, love, and care, Mighty Heart conquered many obstacles to win the 161st-edition of the coveted Queen's Plate, Canada's horse racing jewel and the longest continuously run stakes race in North America. The quest of Mighty Heart in overcoming all odds is a wonderful story. The magic is so eloquently brought to life by the author of this gallant thoroughbred who captured the hearts and souls of an entire country, giving us hope and happiness during a pandemic that rocked our nation.

I have known Jennifer Morrison for decades; Jen is a talented writer who has made Woodbine her home and cherishes its people and their passionate love of racehorses. Jen has accurately portrayed what it meant to the community to have the aptly named Mighty Heart defy the odds for a popular local owner, Larry Cordes, and win the Plate. The story of Cordes will resonate with many, as he weathered personal tragedy but never gave up on his lifelong quest to find success in horse racing.

Mighty Heart was challenged from the beginning, having lost his eye in a paddock accident shortly after birth. When he finally got to the races early in his three-year-old season in New Orleans, he was still learning to manage his vision on the racetrack, and his performance placed his racing future in doubt. Along with this uncertainty, the world was sinking further into the pandemic, forcing the closure of racetracks along with the borders to Canada.

The season at Woodbine Racetrack was delayed by almost two months, with horse racing ultimately being the first sport to return to live-action in the country.

The late start for Woodbine pushed the Queen's Plate back from July to September. In retrospect, the delay gave Mighty Heart a chance to develop and audition for this part as he did not commence his Canadian racing career until the summer.

The story of Larry Cordes and Mighty Heart will absorb you from starting gate to the finish line. Jen Morrison carefully researched and provided a detailed account of Mighty Heart's triumph, which also delivers insight into the critical roles that a racehorse's trainer, groom, exercise rider, and team play in garnering success.

Jen lovingly depicts the arduous path Mighty Heart followed to arrive in front of a nation when we all needed hope and something to smile about. Despite the pandemic, the country experienced a somewhat normal summer in 2020; however, hopelessness surfaced again that fall as COVID-19 numbers returned in an alarming fashion and Mighty Heart's Triple Crown quest arrived on cue to lift our spirits. This feel-good story of the equine star will capture your imagination and dare you to dream.

Much like life, the setbacks in horse racing build the character it takes to persevere. If and when success does arrive, it is that much sweeter, and people in the sport are happy for you because they appreciate the depth of the challenges.

On behalf of the horse racing community, I thank Jen for taking on this project and superbly capturing the horse racing world and the human element that goes with it. Enjoy this book as it takes you on a ride that bursts quickly out of the gate and sustains that pace throughout. For those of us who know and love the majestic sport of horse racing, and those who are being exposed to the sport for the first time through this book, it is the beautiful story of an equine athlete picking up the heart and soul of an entire nation when we all desperately needed a winner.

Jim Lawson, President, Chief Executive Officer,
Woodbine Entertainment, August 2021

Chapter 1:

Pandemic

THE SPRING OF 2020 was just thirty-six hours old when trainer Josie Carroll watched Mighty Heart race erratically around the Fair Grounds racecourse in a maiden turf race on Louisiana Derby day, his head turned awkwardly as he tried to compensate for his missing left eye. It was the biggest afternoon of the Fair Grounds meeting, a New Orleans track that runs from December through March and is a popular spot for Canadian horsepeople to prepare their horses for races in their home country.

Spring's arrival in the sport of Thoroughbred racing is a magical time. The days begin to stretch out, trees slowly fill out with leaves of green, and the hibernating racetracks of the north stir from their long winter's rest.

Many racehorses are also back from a few months of romping in the snow, or if their owners have deeper pockets, time off in the sunshine at farms further south. Dreams of a winning horse in the new year, perhaps the 'big horse,' bubble over for every owner, trainer, jockey, and groom.

For Carroll, late March means the beginning of a winding journey from the south and back to her stable's base at Woodbine in Rexdale, Ontario, Canada's biggest racetrack. Her horses, which she trains for a wide array of Canadian and American owners, have been preparing for a new Woodbine season not only at Fair Grounds but at the idyllic Palm Meadows Training Centre just north of Miami, Florida.

During the winter months, Carroll regularly travels back and forth between Florida and New Orleans to check on her equine students.

When it is time to begin the trek north, many of the two dozen horses are loaded onto vans and will go directly to Ontario, while others will stop with Carroll in Lexington, Kentucky, and the bucolic surroundings of Keeneland racecourse. Its boutique spring meeting is only a few weeks long, but it is an ideal spot for snowbirds to stable or race their horses as they make their way to Woodbine and its mid-April opening day.

On this March 21st afternoon, as she stood trackside at Fair Grounds, it would have been hard for Carroll to find much optimism in the progress of Mighty Heart. She had seen talent in the colt's early training as a two-year-old in 2019, but getting past the colt's quirks, mostly due to that missing left eye, was presenting a challenge.

Mighty Heart, his handsome head with the crooked white blaze cocked sharply to the left, 'blew' the turn in both starts. That is racing parlance for heading to the track's parking lot while his rivals professionally negotiated the race's first turn.

Mighty Heart was one of just a handful of horses owned by one of her newest clients, seventy-six-year-old Lawrence Cordes who built his very successful Lawrcon Electrical and Repair Company in Pickering, Ontario, from the ground up. Cordes fell in love with horses and racing as a young man. He had been dabbling in owning racehorses for almost four decades, but left the sport for almost ten years following a series of tragic events when his wife Connie, daughter Evelyn, and son-in-law Jim Perrin passed away from cancer. Mighty Heart was a product of Cordes's new approach to racing. When he got back into the sport, he wanted to breed his own horse by matching a mare to a stallion.

As a Canadian-bred three-year-old colt, Mighty Heart was one of some one hundred horses in 2020 nominated to Canada's most famous race, the Queen's Plate. Winning the Plate is the dream of every horse owner in the country. And Carroll already had an imposing group of Plate hopefuls, including the unbeaten Corsi, owned by successful Canadian breeder Glenn Sikura and several of his close friends, and the filly Curlin's Voyage, owned by Sikura's brother John and his childhood friends, the Windsor Boys Stable.

But as Mighty Heart was being cooled out from this second, perplexing outing, the colt became the least of Carroll's immediate problems.

The world was under attack by a deadly virus.

A coronavirus, SARS-CoV-2 or COVID-19, detected in December 2019 in Wuhan, China, which caused a dangerous respiratory illness, had been declared a global pandemic by the World Health Organization on March 11. At first, it seemed to be a matter of washing hands and steering clear of travellers, but the cruel, contagious disease was spreading fast, attacking the vulnerable and filling hospitals faster than cities could handle. Not since the Spanish Flu of 1918 had a virus run this rampant over the world.

Not only did Carroll learn that businesses around the world had already begun to shut down, but the Fair Grounds Racetrack was also shutting down while Keeneland was forced to cancel its upcoming racing dates. It soon became apparent that Woodbine was not going through with its scheduled opening day of April 18th.

Governments were increasingly desperate to keep people away from each other to stop the spread. No large gatherings were allowed: bars, restaurants, and movie theatres were closed. No malls or stores, hair salons or gyms could open, and workplaces sent employees home.

Professional sports had already been cancelled.

The stock market crashed dramatically. International borders closed.

"It's time to come home," were the daunting words from Canada's Prime Minister Justin Trudeau for citizens who were out of the country.

Normal life was gone, and no one knew when it was coming back.

"Terribly worried," was how Carroll described her reaction to the news around her. "I had horses in New Orleans and horses in Florida that I had to get home. I had largely an all-Canadian crew that I had brought down to both places and had to make sure they got home safely."

The paperwork—particularly, health certificates for horses—was one of the first hurdles for Carroll and other Canadians seeking to send horses back to Ontario.

For horses to cross borders, in this case, Canadian-based horses returning from the U.S., they must be thoroughly checked by a veterinarian (vets) and test negative for any communicable diseases within thirty days of travel. The vets then submit the paperwork to the United States Department of Agriculture.

"State offices were overwhelmed; some had already shut down because of the pandemic," said Carroll.

"Getting health certificates for some twenty-five horses was quite problematic and very stressful."

The frantic race for the border not only led to backlogs in paperwork but, in many instances, ordering vans to ship horses north became a game of hurry-up-and-wait; there were simply not enough to handle the sudden rush.

Carroll's fellow Woodbine trainers Steven Chircop and his cousin Kevin Attard were stabled at Gulfstream Park in Hallandale, not far from Miami. They were also in scramble mode.

"All of a sudden, things got scary, and people were dying," said Chircop. "We heard about the travel ban, and it was a mad rush for us to organize vans and health papers, but everything was backed up."

Chircop and Attard drove back home together from Florida, and their phones never stopped buzzing.

"Our owners and our staff wanted to know what was going on," said Chircop. "We had to keep checking social media to get updates on what was happening back home. There were even rumours about horses being considered non-essential and that they might not be allowed back into Canada."

Attard, whose large stable of horses included the reigning Canadian Horse of the Year Starship Jubilee, had already sent his diabetic father and trainer Tino home, concerned for his health.

"Nobody had been through something like this before," said Attard. "I just wanted to be back in my own country with our own health care and be safe."

Jim Lawson, the man at the helm of Woodbine Entertainment, which owns Woodbine and the Woodbine Mohawk Park Standardbred track in Campbellville, Ontario, already had his management staff on high alert after that fateful day of March 11th when a global pandemic was declared.

It was a day he will never forget.

"I was sitting in my living room that evening, watching some sports, when it cut away to a scene of NBA basketball players at a Utah Jazz-Oklahoma City Thunder game being whisked off the court," recalled Lawson. "The game had not started, but an announcement was made, and the game was postponed."

Word came out in minutes that a Jazz player had tested positive for COVID-19.

"I said 'oh my god' and knew this was going to have repercussions," said Lawson. "We swung into action pretty darn fast after that."

Woodbine's backstretch, which had opened up for horses to begin training for the season two weeks earlier, was put in lockdown. Protocols were put in place that included bolstered security at the barn area's entrance and only essential staff were permitted in the barns with those workers having to be screened by emergency service workers.

Masks and social distancing in the Woodbine barn area were strictly enforced at the outset of the COVID-19 pandemic. Photo by Michael Burns.

The screening process started with questions as to a person's current health and would soon include daily monitoring of everyone's temperatures.

Anyone who had symptoms of any kind of illness was turned away. A COVID-19 positive test result could shut down training and racing immediately. The Horsemen's Benevolent and Protective Association (HBPA) bought hundreds of masks and distributed them to essential stable workers who were already on the Woodbine backstretch. Mask wearing and social distancing of six feet between workers proved to be a challenge.

"We fought that all year," said Sue Leslie, president of the Ontario division of the HBPA that represents horsepeople at Woodbine and Fort Erie. "We had to regularly send out memos to members reminding them that protocols had to be followed or they risked endangering the racing season."

Jockeys, their agents, and horse owners were not allowed to enter the barn area. Meanwhile, the Canada/U.S. border was set for closure, but not before van loads of horses began to arrive from south of the border. Strict rules were in place that allowed only Woodbine workers to unload the horses and handle equipment; van drivers had to stay in their vehicles.

Some grooms, exercise riders, and hotwalkers who were working for Carroll, Attard, Chircop, and many other Canadian trainers in the U.S., usually live in the dormitories on-site during the Woodbine season, but weren't allowed on the premises, having to go into quarantine for fourteen days.

Leslie and her small staff at the HBPA were thrown into the middle of chaos. They were on the phone fielding questions each day and most nights. Were Canadian horsepeople going to be stranded in the U.S.? Was the insurance provided to them by the HBPA still valid for COVID-19? Once horsepeople, who lived in Woodbine's dorms, got back to Canada, where would they quarantine?

"So much was happening at once, and we were going by instincts, really," said Leslie. "We had to find places for more than two dozen grooms, hotwalkers and exercise riders who had to quarantine and had nowhere to go. And when we tried to line up hotel rooms in the area, the hotel management soon figured out what was happening, and they didn't want any horsepeople there."

Lawson, a lawyer by profession, sports executive, former professional hockey player, and—like his late father Mel—a horse owner and breeder, had to make tough decisions regarding hundreds of Woodbine

Entertainment staff who had been readying for the opening of the racing season. With the prospect of the season being delayed, most of the food and beverage department that oversees half a dozen restaurants and bars at the track were laid off. Ontario Lottery and Gaming was forced to close Casino Woodbine, which takes up the eastern portion of the track.

Woodbine Entertainment's President and CEO Jim Lawson. Photo by Michael Burns.

"We had to pull back immediately to preserve our capital and keep people safe," said Lawson. "We were forcing front line workers to be there every day to take temperatures; meanwhile, we had more people shipping in every day from the U.S."

In emergency discussions with the province's health leaders and Premier Doug Ford, Lawson and Leslie emphasized that some eight hundred horses already on the backstretch needed essential workers to care for them.

Horsepeople were eventually classified as essential, but horse racing was not.

In early April, Lawson announced the inevitable; the Woodbine season would not start on April 18th and no prospective start date was on the table. By that time, the world's most famous horse race, the Kentucky

Derby, traditionally held on the first Saturday in May, had been postponed to the first Saturday in September.

And the longest, continuously run stakes race in North America, the Queen's Plate at Woodbine, was in danger of not being held at all. Scheduled for June 27th, the 161st running of Canada's most famous race was postponed indefinitely.

COVID-19 ravaged long-term care homes, and deaths in the country reached nearly two thousand by mid-April.

Millions of people lost their jobs as businesses shut down, and the Canadian government rolled out aid packages such as the Canadian Emergency Response Benefits for citizens who lost work.

Unemployment in Canada was at a near-record of thirteen percent.

When Mighty Heart and his fellow barn mates arrived in Ontario, Woodbine allowed only light training; horses could be taken out to the track for a light jog or slow gallop.

Training racehorses at Fort Erie racetrack while horsepeople waited to find out when, or if, racing would begin. Photo by Laurie Langley.

With the restriction to training in place at Woodbine, Cordes decided to send Mighty Heart to Steve and Kathleen Kemp's Ballycroy Training Centre in Loretto, about forty minutes north of Woodbine. Mighty Heart arrived at the Kemp's farm on April 3rd and trained on their dirt track with veteran Woodbine jockey Gary Boulanger, who put Mighty Heart through his paces.

Some owners and trainers elected to pack up their horses and send them to nearby farms as the uncertainty about racing was growing. The majority stuck it out.

But frustration was growing.

Owners were getting antsy; bills were piling up. Trainers charge as much as $100 per day to train a horse, including feed, equipment, and staff payroll. Since horses were not getting a chance to have timed workouts or get into racing shape, it would take even longer to prepare the horses.

Backstretch workers were deemed essential by the Ontario government officials to care for thousands of racehorses at Ontario's tracks. Photo by Laurie Langley.

There was the rub.

"I was reluctant, and to be honest, nervous to predict when we might be able to race," said Lawson. "I wanted horsepeople to understand that we were operating the backstretch to provide stabling and care for the livestock, which was deemed an essential business under the Provincial Government's Declaration of Emergency. We had only essential Woodbine Entertainment staff working to operate the backstretch under these conditions. But we needed to be respectful of the Government's protocols."

Making matters more frustrating for local horsepeople was major tracks in Florida and Arkansas, Gulfstream Park and Oaklawn, continued with their winter race meetings, albeit without fans. And little-known tracks such as Will Rogers Downs in Oklahoma and Fonner Park in Grand Island, Nebraska, were also racing and suddenly in the sports betting spotlight. Fonner Park landed on the pages of the *New York Times* as simulcast wagering totals on its races soared.

Horse racing in the U.S. was the only professional sport taking place even as COVID-19 cases, and deaths in that country continued to climb at a rapid pace. Total cases worldwide reached three million and more than half a million people had perished.

As Woodbine racing dates started to be cancelled, the next mission for the various racing organizations was to get some money back into the pockets of owners who were paying for horses at the track.

Woodbine, the HBPA, Ontario Racing (which oversees Thoroughbred, Standardbred and Quarter Horse racing in the province), and the Ontario Lottery and Gaming Corporation had cram sessions to put a relief plan in place using purse money that was not going to be paid out for missed racing days.

The criteria to receive a stipend of $1,500 per horse was seemingly simple. The horse had to be in the care of an Ontario-based trainer with a completed stall application (along with other information) to verify the horse was a resident of Ontario set to race in 2020.

"We knew we had to get money into the hands of owners who had to pay trainers, who had to pay staff, and we didn't even know when or if racing would start," said Leslie. "Bless the owners that kept horses at Woodbine during all the uncertainty," she added. "But we had to go through hundreds of applications for every horse, one by one, and some horses weren't even named yet."

The overwhelming number of applications led to many weeks of delays before Ontario Racing could issue cheques to owners for lost racing time in April and May.

Upon returning to Canada, Josie Carroll settled into her Mississauga home with husband/exercise rider Charlie Nash for a two-week quarantine. It was unfamiliar and somewhat frustrating territory for her as a hands-on trainer who rarely misses a day at the barn to prepare her horses.

And then disaster struck. Her leading Queen's Plate hopeful, Corsi, was out for a morning gallop on the Woodbine main track and was t-boned by a rank horse from another stable and was seriously injured.

"I got the call that Corsi had been run into by another horse, and he might have to be put down," remembered Carroll. "They thought his shoulder was broken, but it was hard for me to assess the situation as I couldn't leave the house."

Corsi survived, but it appeared his promising career was over.

When Carroll was finally able to return to Barn 39, she got to work going over each of her dozens of trainees from head to hoof.

There were over one thousand horses in light training on the Woodbine backstretch when the province of Ontario extended the state of emergency to late April but there were indications that plans to open the economy were in the works.

That isn't to say that the COVID-19 virus spread was dissipating. The epicentre of the virus was still in long-term care homes, some of which lost three-quarters of their residents. Positive cases numbered about five hundred each day but appeared to have peaked.

Lawson was cautiously optimistic that racing could begin in the early summer and gave the green light for trainers to 'work' their horses, increase their training again, on May 1st. Jockeys were also allowed on the backstretch to work their prospective mounts as long as they didn't enter any barns.

A few days after full training opened again, Lawson received a surprising phone call from Premier Ford's office: horse racing was on the list of businesses that could resume during Phase One of the gradual re-opening of

Ontario. Woodbine's opening day was set for June 6th, while Standardbred racing could start the previous night. Quarter Horse racing at Ajax Downs, just east of Toronto, would begin a week later.

Fans and owners would not be permitted, and just two people were allowed to accompany each horse to the paddock to be saddled for a race. But racing was getting a chance to open, and that was a relief to the thousands who worked in the industry.

Woodbine would not be the first Canadian track to re-open, however. Plucky little Assiniboia Downs in Winnipeg, Manitoba, under the guidance of its determined CEO Darren Dunn, was able to begin its meeting on May 25th, just two weeks later than usual.

Dunn had to do some nifty manoeuvring with his track, as the 140 VLT machines, along with the popular food and beverage areas, were shut down. Fans and owners were not permitted, and masks and social distancing were strictly enforced. He tweaked the racing schedule so races could be held on consecutive weekday nights, allowing more customers to watch and wager through simulcast networks. He called it his "cyber meet."

The response was stunning. Without hockey, basketball, baseball, or football, sports and betting-starved fans poured money on Winnipeg races, the track getting more attention on social media than it ever had.

Six races on opening night lured over $1 million in bets, and much of it through Woodbine's online Horseplayer Interactive (HPI) betting platform—a 343% increase from opening day a year earlier.

That momentum would continue through Assiniboia's fifty-day meeting, ending the season with a staggering total of $63 million in wagering, dwarfing the 2019 total of just over $12 million. Dunn was quick to emphasize that his track, much like Nebraska's Fonner Park, does not make much money through simulcast wagering, receiving just a small share of the amount with the bulk going to Woodbine's HPI. The on-track wagering from fans plus concessions are the bread and butter for those tracks.

When Woodbine finally opened on June 6th, it was a sunny, warm summer day, though an eerie scene. The cavernous grandstand, large enough to hold thirty thousand fans, was closed. With just a groom and a trainer allowed to accompany each horse the races were run in near silence. Only the faint race call of track announcer Robert Geller would add a bit of excitement to a fighting finish.

In fact, Woodbine issued a seven-page race-day protocol document detailing screening processes, where horsepeople could stand to watch their horse race, along with a host of other restrictions.

No washrooms were available.

The jock's room was re-calibrated: saunas, steam rooms, and the icebox, along with other amenities, were shut down. In turn, the Alcohol and Gaming Commission of Ontario allowed up to eight pounds in overweight for riders.

As the summer went on and people spent most of their time outdoors, the province slowly reopened the economy. Restaurants, gyms, libraries, and hair salons were back in business, and new COVID-19 cases totalled less than one hundred a day.

With the return of racing at Woodbine, the Queen's Plate was pencilled in for September 12th, a week after the Kentucky Derby. It was exciting news for every owner and trainer of a Canadian-bred three-year-old, particularly those who needed a bit more time to develop and train their prospects.

No one wanted to put a positive spin on the horrific virus that changed every person's life on the planet, but for grooms, hotwalkers, owners, and trainers who make their living in the racing industry, the Plate dream offered a bright light in dark times.

Mighty Heart fit that profile, although Cordes had not been entirely convinced his one-eyed guy was of that calibre. Cordes and Carroll would know a lot more on July 11th, when Mighty Heart was set to make his Woodbine debut.

Chapter 2:

Larry

LARRY CORDES CELEBRATED HIS seventy-sixth birthday on May 27, 2020. He is quick to point out that May 27 is also the birthdate of the most famous Thoroughbred in Canadian history, Northern Dancer, the first Canadian-bred horse to win the Kentucky Derby. The 'Dancer' ended his career with an easy win in the 1964 Queen's Plate and went on to be the most influential stallion in modern racing.

Northern Dancer was born in Oshawa, Ontario, at Edward Plunkett Taylor's Windfields Farm in 1961. He was bay-coloured, small in stature but powerfully built, and had a crooked white blaze down his face and three white feet.

The same birth date aside, Cordes likely could have never predicted that in 2020 his own smallish but strong bay colt would also go on to racing glory.

"I am definitely a believer in fate," said Cordes about sharing his birth date with the great Canadian horse. "When I found out later that Northern Dancer was born on the same day as me, I thought it was pretty great."

As Mighty Heart started up his spring training at Woodbine in those early months of 2020, when the COVID-19 pandemic hit, Cordes moved into the home of his daughter Angela and her adult daughters Jennifer and Megan. Cordes had been living in Port Perry, in the home of his partner, Kimberley

Rutchsmann for twelve years. Though not easily unnerved by any challenge, he made the tough decision to move out as Rutchsmann, a long-term care worker, was at risk of being exposed to COVID-19 every day.

And Cordes is no stranger to loss. Not by a long shot.

In a span of little over five years, from 1999–2005, cancer claimed the life of Connie, his wife of four decades; his oldest daughter Evelyn; and Angela's husband Jim, both just 34 years old.

That amount of loss for one family is unfathomable.

"Five years of unbelievable sadness," Cordes said, his voice trailing off. "I almost gave up my business, gave up racing and my horses. I almost gave up living."

But Connie would not have it. Her final words, he said, saved his life.

"'I am okay, don't worry about me, I'm going home.' That is what she said to me. She said she was going to her meet her mother again and a brother she never met who died during World War II in the caves of Malta. That got me through. Who knows where I would have ended up without her saying that."

His son Darin had to step in and steer the business as his dad grieved. "He took it super hard, of course. He wasn't thinking straight for a while, but that was understandable," said Darin.

With the pandemic taking hold of the world in the spring of 2020, Cordes played it safe and moved north from Port Perry.

Not that Cordes is the kind of man who has ever stayed idle for long. He frequents the Lawrcon office several days a week or travels somewhere in the province on business. He spends time with any horses he may have at the Ballycroy Farm (and later, the property he leased in June 2021 for Angela and his granddaughters to keep their horses).

The move to Uxbridge did give him time to do one big task that he had been putting off for two decades; sifting through dozens of boxes of childhood mementos and photos.

***

Frank and Evelyn Cordes, Larry's parents, lived in the small, northern Ontario town of Penetanguishene (pen-ah-tang-gwi-sheen), nestled near a long bay inlet off Georgian Bay some one hundred kilometres north of Toronto.

Landed by European explorer, Étienne Brûlé, of New France, 'Penetang' —its full name stems from Wyandot and Abenaki dialect meaning "land of the rolling sands" for its many beaches—is considered one of the oldest towns in Canada, west of Quebec City.

Brûlé had been sent by Samuel de Champlain, governor of New France, seeking fur trading contracts with the Hurons. De Champlain would soon arrive in the area and would join forces with the Hurons to battle the Iroquois in the fur trade.

In later years, Penetang had a naval base and was home to military pensioners and farmers.

The Cordes name became prominent in the area as Larry's ancestors arrived from France via Quebec.

In the 1940s, the town had a very large francophone population, and most family sizes were quite large. There was a bit of industry with some foundries, a shoe factory and boat builders. There was even a racetrack on the Penetanguishene property of John Thomas Payette that put Standardbred racing on the map from 1910 to 1940.

"Back in those days, there was nothing there, really," said Cordes. "People who lived there owned several acres of land. There were only a few families where we lived; the Cordes, the Larmands, and Duvals."

Larry was one of six children who would soon move to the burgeoning city of Toronto with its population nearing 700,000. He was just a boy, but Larry was enamoured with the hustle and bustle of streets and businesses, much more so than sitting in a classroom.

"Oh, I was bored to death in school," Cordes laughed. "I was a reasonably quiet boy, but I really had a love for keeping busy. I used to collect newspapers, mattresses, and radiators and sell them. I did errands for people; I was just always on the go."

And it was on the doorstep of that east-end Toronto house on Munro Street where a six-year-old Cordes had an unusual visitor.

"I ran to the door, and there was this fellow with a black-and-white pony, offering to take pictures of the neighbourhood kids," said Cordes. "I was taken with this pony, and from there, my love for horses never left me."

A young Larry Cordes had his picture taken on a pony in Toronto, and he fell in love with horses. Photo courtesy of the Cordes' family.

Speaking of love.

Connie Kiomall had her eye on teenage Lawrence Cordes while both were part of a neighbourhood friend's group that would get together in each other's backyards.

Cordes wasn't exactly of the same mindset at the time. In fact, when he was sixteen, he was dating Connie's older sister. But Connie, a confident, strong-willed girl with a Maltese background, had other ideas.

"Actually, I used to give Connie and the other kids a quarter to get lost so I could sit on the swing with the older sister," he laughed.

"But one day, when Connie was twelve or thirteen at the time, she yelled at me that she would marry me one day. Wouldn't you know, she did."

He was nineteen, and she was sixteen when they wed.

Larry Cordes and his wife Connie. Photo courtesy of the Cordes' family.

By then, an ambitious Cordes had entered the world of electrical repair sales. He was fascinated by machining electric motors, how they worked, and the industry's ever-changing technology. He started working for owners of small shops, learning this trade, but always had the idea that he would start his own business.

A pivotal moment came when he met a business owner who could not get his shop in the black. He was going bankrupt.

True to Cordes' confident personality, he made the man a deal.

"I asked him to give me six months to turn his business around. So, he gave me a car, a guarantee of a salary and expenses, and off I went. By the end of a year, his sales increased, and he was in reasonably good shape. I stayed for two years, and he had a sizable increase in business. By that time, I had educated his son and daughter on how to run the company. So, I said, 'Thank you, I enjoyed helping you' and went into business for myself."

He was twenty-one.

Cordes opened Horizon Electric in an industrial unit in Scarborough, just north of Toronto, and quickly grew his clientele, soon moving to larger workspaces as the business rapidly grew. The company became known as Lawrcon, which he named for himself and Connie.

In 1988, he built his own plant in Pickering that became one of the largest in the province, offering services of machine repair, rewinding of motors, and machining. Currently, he also has a satellite division in Peterborough.

"We're pretty much a household name in the heavy industry in Ontario," said Cordes of his pride and joy that employs a staff of twenty-eight.

"The industry is very rewarding to me. With its ever-changing equipment processes, it has kept my interest. You have to be on top of it, always pursuing the advances in the industry worldwide. And it is not like simply manufacturing a product and people just ordering it; it is a lot of decision-making and knowledge to help your customer become more efficient and more profitable. We offer them more than just repairs and sales. The whole thing was challenging to me, and it still is."

Lawrcon is very much a family-run business with Cordes still playing a major role, Darin and Angela running the company day-to-day, and granddaughter Megan and grandson Kyle now also members of the team.

***

When his business was in the percolating stage, Cordes made time for his horse obsession, particularly his love for Thoroughbred racing. He was always intrigued by betting on the races and studied each horse's record in the *Daily Racing Form* to try and pick a winner.

"My serious interest in horses and the racing aspect began when I was about twenty-three," he said. "I was a bettor all along, and I really liked delving into statistics."

In Toronto in the 1960s, the east end of the Old Woodbine racetrack had been renamed to Greenwood while New Woodbine, a shiny new track, had opened a few years earlier, the pride of its founder E.P. Taylor, the same Taylor who brought Northern Dancer to the world.

Cordes was still that little boy hopping on the pony when Taylor purchased the former Parkwood Stables in Oshawa from Colonel R.S. 'Sam' McLaughlin, founding president of General Motors, in 1950. Taylor had already cut a swath through the business landscape in Ontario. By his early-thirties, he had formed the Brewing Corporation of Ontario, Canadian Breweries, and had control of big companies such as the Dominion stores and Massey Ferguson.

Taylor also had a deep passion for horses and bought his first racehorses in the early 1930s to race for his Cosgrave Stable. Cosgrave morphed into a farm, National Stud Farm, nestled just south of the 401-highway surrounded by York Mills Road, Leslie Street, and Bayview Avenue in Toronto. The name would soon change to Windfields Farm, named for his first stakes winning horse.

Taylor was also instrumental in revamping horse racing in Ontario. As a member of the Ontario Jockey Club (OJC), he set forth a plan to rebuild a waning, corruption-riddled horse racing industry in the province. Under Taylor, the OJC bought up seven tracks in southern Ontario, sold off most, and in 1956, Taylor unveiled the 'giant of the north', Woodbine Racetrack.

What skyrocketed Taylor and his homebred horses to world fame was that May day in 1961 when his mare Natalma gave birth to a colt, a son of Nearctic, who went unsold at his yearling sale for $25,000. That was Northern Dancer.

Northern Dancer in the Kentucky Derby winner's circle in 1964 with his owner and breeder, E. P. Taylor. Photo courtesy of Churchill Downs.

Following his racing career, Northern Dancer solidified his place as the greatest stallion of the twentieth century. He sired dozens of champions and one hundred forty-six stakes winners. His sons went out and became leading sires, and their sons did the same.

Consider this: In January 2020, a study on ten thousand Thoroughbreds was performed by scientists at the University College Dublin and equine science company Plusvital, which found that ninety-seven percent of the genomes traced back to the Dancer. Virtually every starter in the Kentucky Derby today has Northern Dancer blood in their pedigree.

Cordes got a peek at Northern Dancer when the colt was attending his early training lessons at Windfields in Toronto. The youngsters that went unsold from Taylor's yearling consignments would be sent to that farm to prepare for racing.

"I wanted to see what a Thoroughbred farm was all about. I saw all these yearlings in a field and then a little horse that looked like a pony. I asked the farm manager, Peter Poole, who the little one was, and he said he was named Northern Dancer. I got a closer look, and he was built like a tank. He had a chest wider than any horse in the field and a big ass end."

When Taylor hosted his annual yearling sale in 1962, Cordes clearly wanted him to buy him. "I was just young, I didn't have two nickels, but I scraped some money together just for that sale." The bidding went too high for Cordes but not high enough for Taylor, and the Dancer went on to make history for his breeder.

In the mid-1970s, with their business continuing to grow, Larry and Connie's family grew as well. They welcomed their three children, Evelyn, Darin, and Angela, and moved everyone to a bungalow on a small hobby farm in the rural town of Brooklin, Ontario, just a few furlongs north of Windfields Farm.

With the help of friends and family, Cordes built up the property to have a barn, a small racetrack, and paddocks. The animal-loving family soon had a large number of critters living on the property, from chickens and sheep to cows and goats.

"We had all kinds of farm animals," said Angela, who was seven years old at the time. "My dad went to an auction in Stouffville and bought a couple of horses, and we had chickens and sheep. I even had a pet pig that we rescued as the runt of a litter. I will never forget bringing that pet pig home in my mom's Lincoln Town Car."

Horses were a mainstay at the farm, and Cordes' first experience as a racehorse owner came when Connie presented him with a Thoroughbred for his birthday.

"That was pretty much the start of it," said Cordes. "We had some damn good success with that first horse too."

You could ask Cordes about some of his first experiences with owning horses, and he doesn't miss a beat, rhyming off the horses' pedigree and the ups and downs that came with buying it.

"Nellie May, she was an interesting one," said Cordes. "Here was a filly I saw at the local sale by a stallion named Kingwell out of a nothing mare. I had looked at a lot of horses at that sale, and when I saw her, she was this nice, big horse, and her conformation was pretty good. I bought her for $5,500, which was a lot back in 1976."

Nellie May started off well in her racing career, but one morning, in a training session to help her break out of the gate better, she stumbled and broke both her knees.

"We had to put her down, and that was really hard, losing her."

Connie had commissioned artwork of Nellie May that still resides in Cordes' collection at home.

Cordes furthered his love for horse racing with a couple of runners each year, and he even tried his hand in breeding a few of his own, including one that was unexpectedly born on the family farm.

"Dad would go out every morning to feed the horses," said Angela. "We always had a couple there, and one, No Pinching, was in foal and soon to go to a breeding farm to have the foal. One morning, Dad could not understand why the mare was so aggressive to him when he went to feed her. When he went into the stall to change her water, he saw this little head peek out from behind the mare. She had the foal all on her own."

That filly, Frills and Lace, was later sold and went on to win four races in the U.S.

Not only was Larry expanding his knowledge of racing and breeding, but he had become a shrewd horseman. What he did with Evelyn's riding horse, College Fund, during the '70s and early '80s would have likely made some of the greatest horse trainers raise a brow.

He was on a horse-seeking trip to the property of well-known horse importer Alexander Picov in nearby Ajax, whose businesses included a popular saddlery shop and his own Picov Downs, where Sunday Quarter Horse races were a local attraction.

"I was just looking at some horses, mostly to find one for Evelyn to ride. She was such an animal lover and had a connection with them. Squirrels would come up to her, raccoons, you name it."

Picov mentioned that he had a big copper-coloured gelding who had been problematic for his riders with a penchant for dropping to his knees and rolling when someone would climb on his back. To Cordes, it sounded like the Illinois-bred gelding College Fund, originally a pricey purchase by Picov, was not to be trusted.

"'Dad, let me get on him,' Evelyn said to me. I thought it was crazy, but I snapped a lunge line and a lip chain on him and led her around."

Cordes let the lunge line out a bit more before he let go of the line altogether. "She had that horse doing anything she wanted for twenty minutes. Figure-eights, backing up, anything."

Cordes bought the horse and took him home. Little did Cordes know that after the horse settled in at the family farm, Evelyn and Connie had plans of their own for College Fund.

"One day, they came waltzing in the door holding up a set of jockey silks," said Cordes. "Laughing, I said, 'What the hell are those for?'"

The conversation between father and daughter continued:

"We registered him to race at Picov Downs," said Evelyn.

"What are you talking about? He's a riding horse!"

"I want you to train him for the races."

It sounded like the craziest idea in the world. College Fund was already eight years old in 1979, well past the age of most active racehorses. The great Seabiscuit retired from a long career of racing at age seven.

Cordes finally agreed on the condition that his daughter would be out early in the barn to help clean the stall and cool the gelding out after training.

Still, he had his work cut out for him in turning College Fund into a fit and trim racehorse.

College Fund was a bit rotund, some four hundred pounds away from ideal racing weight, not to mention that he had never seen a racetrack or starting gate.

"We jogged him and jogged him around the farm and got about two hundred pounds off him. Then we took him to Picov Downs to see how he would do with the starting gate and, well, a lot of people there were laughing at us. We broke him from the gate and took him home and trained him for three more months."

The following year, on August 3, 1980, at the senior age of nine, College Fund was entered in his first race at Picov Downs.

Incredibly, he galloped to victory.

In fact, College Fund would go on to win four races at Picov Downs and the Markham Fair in a brief but successful career.

RACE 9

7th QUINELLA

3-year-olds and up. Speed Index 69 and under. Purse $370.

POST TIME 5:20 p.m.

	Date	Track	Cond. Class		Purse	Dist.	Win.Tm.	Post	Fin.	Wthr.	Wght.	Jocke
1010	**INNISFREE IVY**				S. M. 1976, by Lee's Blair Bar — Tio's Bars Three							
					Jockey — VINCE BRADLEY							
1					Owner — Sandra Watson							
	July 26	Picov	ft	SI-69u	250	300yd	16.56	1	2pt1⁴⁰	l/c	127	WebsterS
3-1	Jun 21	Picov	gd	SI-69u	500	440yd	23.15	6	4⁶²	l/n	127	Bradley
	Jun 7	Picov	ft	SI-70u	500	350yd	18.74	8	2³⁰	c/c	128	Bradley
	Oct 19	Picov	hy	SI-79u	175	440yd	23.22	1	4⁶¹	l/n	116	Bradley
	Oct 12	Picov	ft	SI-69u	500	440yd	23.19	4	1⁷¹	l/t	116	Bradley
	Sept 27	Markm	ft	SI-70u	200	350yd	18.90	3	3⁶⁵	c/h	118	Radley
1020	**INNISFREE SUSIE**				S. M. 1978, by Lee's Blair Bar — Sue Etta							
					Jockey — GRANT PEARCE							
2					Owner — Innisfree Valley Farm							
	Aug 2	Picov	gd	SI-70u	250	440yd	23.31	5	3⁶³	c/c	125	Pearce
4-1	July 19	Picov	gd	SI-65u	560	400yd	21.47	4	3⁶¹	l/c	125	Pearce
	July 12	Picov	gd	SI-69u	325	300yd	nt	2	2pt1nt	l/c	nr	GreenV
	Jun 28	Picov	gd	SI-69u	400	440yd	23.29	1	1⁶⁰	c/c	125	Pearce
	Jun 14	Picov	ft	SI-65u	325	250yd	13.94	1	4³⁷	l/n	127	GreenV
	Jun 7	Picov	ft	SI-70u	500	350yd	18.74	5	6⁵⁴	c/c	121	McIne
1030	**WHITEVALE KID**				Ro. G. 1977, by Mr. Top Kid — Tara Dial							
					Jockey — TOBY SLATER							
3					Owner — M. & D. Slater							
	July 12	Picov	gd	SI-69u	325	300yd	nt	4	5nt	l/c	nr	Slater
10-1	Oct 12	Picov	ft	SI-69u	500	440yd	23.19	1	6⁶⁹	l/t	123	Kemp
	Oct 4	Markm	ft	SI-69u	350	350yd	18.81	1	4⁶⁶	l/h	123	Kemp
	Oct 2	Markm	ft	SI-69u	450	350yd	nt	4	3nt	l/h	116	McMa
	Sept 27	Markm	ft	SI-59u	500	350yd	19.04	7	1⁶⁴	c/h	116	McMa
	Sept 14	Picov	ft	SI-59u	400	440yd	23.65	5	6⁴⁷	l/n	121	McIn
1040	**COLLEGE FUND**				Ch. G. 1971, by Flashy Dynamo — Leo M Miss							
					Jockey — WAYNE GREEN							
4					Owner — Evelyn Cordes							
	Aug 2	Picov	gd	SI-70u	250	440yd	23.31	1	4¹⁰	c/c	127	Brad
6-1	July 19	Picov	gd	SI-65u	560	400yd	21.47	5	5³⁷	l/c	122	McIr
	Jun 21	Picov	gd	SI-70u	175	300yd	16.58	1	1⁶⁶	l/n	127	Brai
	Oct 19	Picov	hy	SI-60u	500	250yd	14.00	7	5⁴⁰	l/h	120	O'B
	Sept 14	Picov	ft	SI-59u	400	440yd	23.65	4	3⁵⁵	l/n	120	O'B
	Sept 7	Picov	hy	SI-59u	325	400yd	21.44	6	5³³	c/c	121	Sko
1050	**TIGERS LADY REED**				S. M. 1977, by Tuff Tiger Joe — Picks Cherry							
					Jockey — RICK RADLEY							
5					Owner — Bar—H-3 Ranch							
	July 26	Picov	ft	SI-59u	175	300yd	16.67	2	2⁶¹	l/c	120	Ra
7-2	Oct 4	Markm	ft	SI-59u	650	350yd	18.64	7	7⁵⁸	l/h	123	Ba
	Oct 2	Markm	ft	SI-59u	600	350yd	nt	6	3nt	l/h	123	Ba
	Sept 27	Markm	ft	SI-65u	400	350yd	19.04	7	4⁵⁸	c/h	123	Ba
	Sept 14	Picov	ft	SI-69u	124	440yd	23.30	3	4⁴⁹	l/n	124	Bi
	Aug 24	Picov	ft	SI-74u	400	300yd	16.20	4	7⁵⁶	c/n	123	B
1060	**MOONLIGHT LIBERTY**				Ch. M. 1977, by Moonlight Jet — Liberty Lady Leo							
					Jockey — BRUCE SMITHER							

The race-day program from Picov Downs, August 9, 1981, shows College Fund (number four), owned by Evelyn Cordes. Photo by Jennifer Morrison.

A broken blood vessel in his sinus cavity put an end to College Fund's racing career, but once he was fully healed, the lovable gelding and Evelyn went on to thrive in barrel racing events. The two were inseparable for many years until Evelyn got married and moved away from home.

"He was pretty sad when she moved out," said Cordes. "So, we found him a good home with another young girl, and he had a great life. He lived to be twenty-eight."

Horses and racing became a regular family affair for the family. Thoroughbreds took over as the focus on the farm, and a trip to Woodbine to watch the horse races was the norm for the family. Larry and Angela remember virtually every horse that crossed their path in those days, including one filly with a humorous name.

From left to right, Evelyn Cordes, Connie, Angela, Larry, and Darin on Angela's wedding day to her late husband, Jim. Photo courtesy of the Cordes' family.

"My dad bought a nice roan filly at the Woodbine sale one year. He submitted, I think, about fifteen names for her and none of them were accepted by The Jockey Club. He got mad and just submitted Connie's Nightmare, and that is the one they let him have," Angela said, laughing. "I don't think Mom was too impressed."

When the three Cordes children moved out of the Brooklin farm to start their own families, Larry and Connie stayed until the tragic news came that Connie had brain cancer. Soon after, Angela's husband Jim was also felled by the deadly disease and Angela, with two young children at home, cared for Jim while pregnant with their third child. Connie and Jim passed away two years apart.

Larry sold the farm and eventually moved in with Angela in Port Perry, only to find out that Evelyn had cervical cancer. She passed away in 2005.

"It was cruel," said Angela. "But we all had to keep on living for the ones who were with us. You have to keep living for the things you love to do. For Dad, that was his business and his horses."

But by then, Larry had already put horses on the backburner.

He did not race a horse after 2002, and it was nine years before he came back to the sport.

Chapter 3:

The Love of the Horse

"I JUST GOT SO damn discouraged."

Larry got out of horse racing at the turn of the new millennium. Devastated by the loss of Connie, Jim, and then Evelyn, horse racing was not fun anymore. It didn't help that his one-horse stable, Y'all So Pretty, was on a 16-race losing streak through 2002, or that a horse he claimed with his long-time trainer Tino Attard for $25,000 broke his leg in his first workout and had to be put down.

"I just said to myself, 'This can't go on,'" said Cordes. "It was not so much a financial thing, but just plain discouraging. No matter what I did, what I paid for a horse, nothing happened."

However, his passion for the Thoroughbred was too strong for him to give up racing altogether, and he decided to spend a few years studying breeding and successful pedigree nicks.

Larry surrounded himself with every type of Thoroughbred pedigree references, such as annual stallion directories and online pedigree services. He mapped out hypothetical matings. In essence, much like sifting through a horse race to pick a winner, Cordes was 'handicapping' how certain match-ups of stallions worked with mares from various pedigree lines.

"That's why I was away from it for all those years. I wanted to study what the results would be when you breed a certain stallion to a particular mare."

Once he felt he had educated himself enough on some of the more successful breeding nicks, he was anxious to return to Thoroughbred ownership.

"I thought, dammit, I'm going to get back into this thing. I am going to buy a horse based on pedigree and see how that goes. I love the racing game, and I wanted to contribute, but not on a huge scale, just with a couple of mares to breed."

Cordes began scouting some young, unraced horses at a two-year-old sale in 2011 in Ocala, Florida. He was looking for a winning pedigree, and hopefully, a filly he could race and then breed.

He didn't have any luck with buying while the sale was on, but a colt and a filly were offered to him in a package deal after the auction.

The colt was a son of a hot young stallion named Southern Image, who earned $1.8 million in his career. The filly was a daughter of the beautifully-bred stallion City Place, a son of world-class sire Storm Cat, and a grandson of Northern Dancer. Cordes did some bargaining and got the pair for $75,000 American dollars.

Back home at Woodbine that May, Cordes added to his small stable by claiming the filly American Placed, who was racing for a $32,000 selling price for prominent Canadian owners Jim and Susan Hill of Alberta. Claiming races make up the bulk of racing in North America and allow horses to race at their talent level. These races also allow other owners and trainers to purchase the horse right before the race for the set price.

American Placed was a daughter of Kentucky stallion Quiet American, whose son Real Quiet came within a nose of winning the 1998 American Triple Crown. American Placed won by two lengths in her first race for Cordes and trainer Attard, and collected $28,000 in purse money.

That racing season was quite a comeback for Cordes as a horse owner. He owned three horses who won six races and purses in excess of $140,000. The colt by Southern Image, named Hurry Up Alan, would race successfully for Cordes for several seasons, earning almost $300,000 before he was sold to American interests.

Emma's Bullseye, the filly by City Place, was another one of those winners in 2011, and while her racing career was cut short, she would prove to be the best purchase Cordes ever made.

It was a warm July afternoon at Woodbine when Emma's Bullseye went to the post for her first race, a short five-furlong dash for two-year-old fillies. None of the nine entries had raced before, and since Emma's Bullseye and her jockey Justin Stein had drawn post position one in the gate, there were no doubt some anxious moments while waiting for her rivals to get settled at the gate.

Larry and his prized mare, Emma's Bullseye. Photo courtesy of the Cordes' family.

Not many fans bet on Emma's Bullseye; she was 31-to-1 odds and the second-longest shot in the field. When the gates opened and the field was a few strides on their way, it quickly looked like the fans had made a big mistake.

Emma's Bullseye shot to the lead and won by five lengths in a fast time, 57.84. Anyone who bet two bucks to win on her got $64.80 in return.

Unfortunately, Cordes and Attard would never get to see that brilliance again as Emma's Bullseye would emerge from that exciting victory with an injured tendon.

"She showed so much great speed and promise. I spent two-and-a-half years after that win and thousands of dollars trying to get her to race again, but it didn't work out. So, I bred her."

Cordes got to work studying what stallion might be a good match for his speedy filly and was lured to Midas Touch, a British-bred horse with Group 2 stake race success, who had recently arrived in Lexington. This was where Cordes met Gerry and Dana Aschinger, owners of War Horse Place and two people who would later play a pivotal role in the creation of Mighty Heart.

Emma's Bullseye was bred to Midas Touch in the spring of 2014, the start of what would be a memorable year for Cordes in horse racing.

That fall, Cordes claimed a strapping five-year-old gelding named Turkish who was showing signs that he was getting better with each race. Cordes paid $40,000 for Turkish, and Attard sent the horse out to win in his second start for the owner. Then, on the last day of racing of the 2014 Woodbine season, Turkish won the gruelling 1 3/4 mile Valedictory Stakes, a Grade 3 event, after a hard-fought battle to the wire, winning by a long neck under top rider Emma-Jayne Wilson.

It was the first stakes victory for Cordes, and he won his biggest purse, a hefty $90,000.

He was beaming as he posed with Turkish in the winner's circle.

"He's a wonderful horse, and it's a privilege to be associated with him, Tino, and Emma," Cordes said after the race. "This is my first stakes win in forty-five years in the business."

His stable continued to do well for the next two years; Turkish was retired, but one of his newly claimed horses, the filly Trigger Finger, looked like a nice prospect.

But when the filly became mired in a long winless streak in the summer of 2016, Cordes made a change in trainers for his small stable.

He selected Josie Carroll, a two-time Queen's Plate winner and regarded as one of the best trainers in the country.

The first horse that Carroll was put in charge of for Cordes was Emma's Bullseye's first foal, Touch of Emma, who was born in 2015. The filly needed some extra time to get to the races, and she made her first start late in 2017. It didn't take her long to find the winner's circle as she won her second career race in the same fashion as her mum, sprinting away to the lead early in the race. Touch of Emma was Cordes' only horse to race in 2017, and she would go on to win two more races before she was claimed from a race by a new owner in 2019.

There was another offspring of Emma's Bullseye coming up through the ranks in 2019.

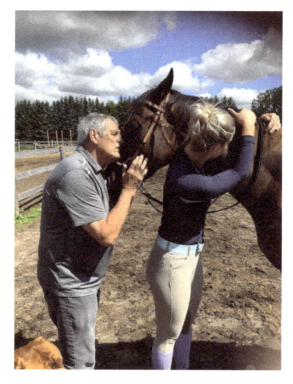

Larry and granddaughter Jennifer share a special moment with In Memory of Floyd, who was retired from the track to become a riding horse and the family pet.

In Memory of Floyd, a friendly, brown fellow was the second foal of the mare, born in 2016 and a product of a breeding between the mare and the Kentucky stallion Istan, whom Cordes was partial to since he was the sire of Turkish.

In Memory of Floyd had all the tools to be a top-class runner, but he also came with a delicate frame.

"Floyd ran so well in 2019, he made about $100,000 [CAD], but we found he had a chip in his ankle. When our vet suggested we take it out, we did take him for surgery, but he eventually developed severe arthritis. Rather than entering him in races and putting him at risk, I decided he had been too good to me, so I retired him, and he became my riding horse."

The breeding process in Thoroughbred racing can be fulfilling and exhilarating: there is no greater thrill than picking out a stallion for your mare and watching that foal go on to racing stardom. It can also be fraught with frustration and heartbreak. Maybe the mare does not get in foal, loses the foal, or worse, mare or foal suffers from a serious injury while playing around in the paddocks. Plenty of patience and luck is needed. The earliest a Thoroughbred is of age to race is two, making it at least a four-year wait until your foal makes his first start.

Breeding racehorses is big business for thousands of farms worldwide who raise them to sell at the high-profile yearling sales, such as those in Kentucky, while Canadian breeders point to sales in their province. Others, such as legendary Sam-Son Farms, founded by Milton, Ontario's, Ernie Samuel in the 1960s, breed to race these offspring themselves.

All that studying of breeding and pedigree nicks had certainly started to pay dividends for Cordes, but the jackpot was still to come.

Before either one of his first couple of homebreds made their first start at the races, Cordes worked on finding the third mate for Emma's Bullseye for the 2016 breeding season. He had been tipped off by his Kentucky friends Gerry and Dana Aschinger at War Horse Place that a new stallion at their Lexington farm may be of interest.

Dramedy was not your typical, commercially attractive stallion, as he was a late-developing horse who excelled in longer races on the grass. Traditionally, the precocious, speedy studs; or Kentucky Derby; or Breeders'

Cup Classic winners get the most attention from breeders seeking the best possible price for a sales yearling.

Dramedy was the Kentucky stallion Cordes picked to breed with Emma's Bulleye for her third foal. Photo by Louise E. Reinagel.

That is not to say that Dramedy did not have an illustrious pedigree and a handsome frame to match. Foaled in 2009 at the high-profile WinStar Farm in Kentucky, Dramedy traced back to the French-bred La Troienne, considered one of the great broodmares in twentieth-century America. His female family was loaded with top-class racehorses and successful producing mares. His half-brother, Bluegrass Cat, like Dramedy, was produced from the mare, She's a Winner, and earned over $1.7 million on the track.

And Dramedy's sire, Distorted Humor, was well on his way to establishing himself as one of the leading stallions of the millennium.

Oh, and his pedigree traced back to none other than Northern Dancer, who appeared twice in his fourth generation.

WinStar raced Dramedy once, late in his three-year-old season, and he won a one-mile dirt race at New York's Aqueduct racetrack by a determined head. He was offered for sale soon after at a Kentucky auction and was purchased by Dustin Moore and Chad Calvert's CTR Stables for $185,000.

But the horse would not race again for sixteen months, and after four races for his new owners, he was entered in another sale.

"Dustin was a client of ours, so the horse had been here on our farm during his lay-up," said Dana Aschinger. "They ran him a few times, but the horse would be sore, and we could never find anything wrong with him."

Gerry Aschinger would end up buying Dramedy for friends John and Marlene James of Oklahoma for $70,000, and the horse promptly went out and won his first start, a minor race at Delaware Park, for the new owners.

Aschinger eventually took over the training of Dramedy, but found the horse was having trouble coming out of the starting gate in a timely manner.

"One day, a girl came by our farm to visit the horse," recalled Dana. "She had worked with him as a youngster and remembered he had injured his hip as a yearling. We realized that he had some arthritis in that area, so Gerry worked with him and found the horse did better with a good warm-up before his races."

In the spring of 2015, Dramedy put it all together and won the $250,000 Elkhorn Stakes, a Grade 2 event on the Keeneland turf course, earning the James's $150,000.

Dramedy raced three more times, but suffered a condylar fracture in one of his legs, requiring surgery at the famed Rood & Riddle Equine Hospital.

Once recovered, Dramedy joined the Aschingers at War Horse Place to begin his stallion career at $7,500 per breeding. He was one of some three hundred stallions in North America that mare owners could select from in the spring of 2016.

"My husband was incredible at doing nick patterns for mares and stallions and studying pedigrees," said Aschinger. "He was a big believer in this horse; so was Mr. James."

The Aschingers were also followers of the 'big heart theory' or the 'X Factor' theory named for the large heart gene that is located on the x chromosomes, one of which is in male horses and two in females. In racehorses, a large heart, in essence, makes a better racehorse. Many famous racehorses have been studied for heart size, including the great Secretariat, American Triple Crown winner in 1973 who had a twenty-two-pound heart, well above the normal size of eight to ten pounds.

Studies have shown that should a mare have a marker for a large heart size on both x chromosomes, they tend to have a strong record of producing progeny with large hearts.

"And all four of the mares on Dramedy's female family had that double marker chromosome," said Aschinger.

Suzanne Smallwood, president of the Lexington-based Equix, uses scientific data such as equine biomechanics and cardio efficiency to determine the racing performance potential of yearlings and two-year-olds. Her company uses ultrasounds to scan the heart's left chamber, the output valve, recording consistent beats and taking measurements when the chamber is in the expanded state (diastolic) and when the chamber contracts (systolic). A calculation for 'stroke volume' comes from such a measurement indicating how much blood is being pumped per beat.

"[Dramedy] showed excellent stroke volume and function," said Smallwood. "Such a heart tends to give the horse the endurance needed for racing at a variety of distances, in particular those of a mile and beyond. As you would expect, the majority of elite runners have very good heart capacity."

Cordes was sold on Dramedy.

"I decided to take a shot and breed Emma's Bullseye to him," said Cordes. "They didn't seem to be getting many mares to him, but this horse could run a distance, and my mare was a short distance horse. And his female pedigree line? It was the best anywhere."

Larry, Angela, and Jennifer placed Emma's Bullseye in a van (they often did their own horse transporting) and drove her to the Aschingers in the spring of 2016. When the mare was pronounced in foal to Dramedy, she was sent to Vera Simpson and Mike Dubé's Curraghmore Farm in Waterdown, Ontario, to foal the following spring.

Cordes had heard a lot about Curraghmore, a ninety-acre family-run nursery and one of the most respected Thoroughbred farms in the province. It was at Curraghmore where some of the most successful owners in Canada had placed their mares to foal, stallions to stand, or racehorses to get some rest time. For over thirty-five years, Curraghmore was the home of horses owned by Richard Kennedy, Eugene Melnyk, Charles Fipke, and the late Mel Lawson, a member of the Canadian Horse Racing Hall of Fame whose three-time champion mare Eternal Search is buried on the farm. Lawson's son Jim, president of Woodbine Entertainment, has continued his father's tradition by keeping his own horses at Curraghmore.

Simpson, who learned her horsemanship at a young age through the British Horse Society Pony Club, came with a reputation of innate knowledge of equine nutrition, the hallmark of Curraghmore. Dubé, a former pipe organ builder, was a skilled woodworker who kept the farm in pristine order and whose calm disposition made him an expert horse handler.

Simpson was immediately impressed with Larry and his family's passion for their horses. "I met Larry in the fall of 2016 when he was seeking a place for Emma's Bullseye to have her foal by Dramedy," said Simpson. "They do all their vanning of their horses and make it a family outing. You could see how much they loved their horses."

Vera Simpson and Mike Dubé of Curraghmore Farm in Waterdown, Ontario,
where Mighty Heart was born. Photo by Dave Landry.

Emma's Bullseye made her presence known at Curraghmore almost immediately. "She was a well-built, very substantial mare with a tough personality. She had no problem pushing her human handlers around."

Everything was in place for Emma's Bullseye as she made Curraghmore her home for the year. And on April 5, 2017, at 8:45 p.m., Emma's Bullseye, with the help of Simpson and Dubé, produced a bold, chocolate-coloured colt by Dramedy.

Chapter 4:

A Colt is Born

IT TOOK ONLY TWENTY minutes for the colt to stand on his wobbly legs, with the occasional fall into the soft bed of straw as he learned to balance. An hour later, he was nursing on his dam's colostrum, the first milk produced by a mare. With the consistency of honey, colostrum contains antibodies from the mare's blood that was not passed onto the foal while pregnant. Such antibodies are then passed on at the first nursing, which gives the foal the immunity it needs early in life.

"When a foal successfully receives colostrum through nursing, it is called passive transfer," explained Vera Simpson. "A foal's digestive system can only break down and utilize the colostrum in the first twenty-four hours of life, with the most effective absorption between six and eight hours from birth. It's important they begin nursing aggressively."

Each foal has blood drawn within the first twelve hours to perform an immunoglobulins G (IgG) test that determines the amount of IgG—the most common antibody—that has been absorbed into the foal's bloodstream. Amounts greater than four hundred to eight hundred milligrams per decilitre are considered sufficient levels, although eight hundred is considered the 'gold standard' level, meaning the mare has passed along a good amount of antibodies.

"Emma's Bulleye's colt had a level of 1,843 mg/dl; not totally rare that it was that high, but it makes you feel good that the foal has lots of protection," said Simpson.

Each foal born at Curraghmore also receives hyperimmune plasma intravenously to protect them from the Rhodococcus equine pneumonia, a bacteria that "sits in the soil, mostly in warmer climates" and has now been detected in Ontario, Simpson noted.

Now fully protected from disease, the foal can discover the outside world in the paddocks with his mother and other newborns. "Tough racehorses are made from living outside as much as they can as young horses, not in a stall," said Simpson. "We put our heart and soul into making sure every foal born on our farm grows up strong and healthy. And you treat every single one of them as if they are all going to be Queen's Plate winners."

A young Mighty Heart, before his paddock accident, with his dam Emma's Bullseye at Curraghmore Farm. Photo by Dave Landry.

Six weeks later, while Emma's Bullseye and her colt were spending the days outside romping in the lush pastures of Curraghmore, Larry and granddaughter Jennifer were on a spring trip to the south. Traditionally, he heads to Florida in April or May to take in some races at Gulfstream Park near Miami and, if one of his horses happens to be wintering there, drops in for a visit.

Occasionally, he didn't come home empty-handed.

"I think my dad is a horse hoarder," Angela laughed. "Just look at the riding horse I have now: Dad fell in love with her on a trip to Gulfstream several years ago."

Cordes was feeding mints and carrots to a filly named Flashy Gayego in the barn of his trainer Tino Attard and son Kevin at Gulfstream one recent winter. They told him the owners didn't want her.

"She had lost her first race by thirty-five lengths or something, and Dad called me and said, 'I think I have a nice hunter prospect for Megan,' my youngest daughter. I said, 'Dad, no, not another horse.'"

The filly, who later became known as Beverly, was soon on her way to Canada.

"He's such a sucker for horses; they are his passion," said Angela. "I guess they are for all of us."

On that mid-May Florida vacation in 2017, Larry and Jennifer also treated themselves to a cruise.

They were likely planning for dinner on the evening of May 19th when Angela suddenly called. There had been an accident with Emma's Bullseye's colt, and his left eye was badly damaged.

"Vera called me trying to get hold of Dad," recalled Angela. "No one knows how it happened, but she said the eye needed to come out. I felt sad for my dad. He was trying to develop a nice horse and had only just started concentrating on breeding his own. But he was not having the luck he wanted or what we had hoped for him."

That evening at Curraghmore was supposed to be like any other; the mares and foals were brought in to the barn for the night.

The herd had been fed at lunchtime, and nothing was untoward, but the scene was much different at day's end.

"Well, he came bounding up to the gate with everyone and wasn't acting any differently," said Simpson. "But then I saw his left eye. Here is this poor little foal with his eye badly damaged—it was horrible."

Simpson quickly called her long-time farm veterinarian and friend Dr. Keith Colquhoun to look at the colt. He didn't hesitate: the colt had to be sent to the Ontario Veterinary College (OVC) at the nearby University of Guelph.

The little colt was loaded on a van with his mother. Within hours, it was determined that the damage to the eye was too severe to save and surgery was performed to remove it. The veterinary notes from OVC read:

Foal was bright and alert, sedated for examination. Left eye had ruptured, protrusion of the iris through the cornea, soft tissue swelling around eye socket and hemorrhaging around interior chamber. Left eye was removed under general anaesthetic.

Four days later, the foal returned to Curraghmore with a bandage around his head to protect the sutures around his eye socket. "He was on stall rest, his bandages changed every couple of days, and then he was turned out in a small paddock for fourteen days," said Simpson. "You would never know by his behaviour that he had no eye; he acted exactly the same."

Larry's granddaughter Jennifer remembers the first time she saw the young colt, soon after the surgery.

"When we went to Vera's farm together after he was born, it was the first time I had ever seen a horse with a missing eye," said Jennifer. "It was very freaky to me, and it was a bit sad, too. I don't think Poppy was too sure the colt would amount to anything as a racehorse."

So, what happened that day in the paddock? Simpson said it is impossible to know.

"Who knows what happened. I could see him flying around the paddock with the other mares and foals and having fun, causing some trouble. It's likely he got kicked accidentally. He was a tough little guy, and his personality eventually started to stand out. It didn't take us long to say he's just like his mother," she laughed.

Megan agreed. "He was just a little a-hole as a foal. On one of my visits to the farm, he decided to lunge at me. He was a troublemaker."

There was some discussion between Cordes, Simpson, and the vets about whether to put in a prosthetic eye, but as the colt had plenty of growing to do, the risk of complications was too high.

What Cordes was told, which offered him a glimpse of hope, was because the eye had been removed so early in the colt's life, the little fellow would probably not notice anything was different.

"We wondered what his future would be and how it would impact him as a racehorse," said Angela.

"But as I told Dad, I had heard there had been some successful horses with one eye."

She was right.

Vision-impaired racehorses are rare, but there have been a few very good equine athletes that were missing vision in one eye.

In 1911, there was an unlikely victory by Glenside in the famous Grand National Steeplechase at Aintree, England. Frank Bibby's one-eyed long-shot, who had been trounced in the previous year's Grand National, and was plagued by breathing issues, managed to outstay what few horses did not fall at fences to win by a reported twenty lengths.

In the 1950s, One-Eyed King, trained by the great horseman Woody Stephens, won two editions of the important Donn Handicap at Gulfstream Park in Florida.

Cassaleria was the first one-eyed horse to run in the Kentucky Derby. While he was only thirteenth in the 1982 Derby, Cassaleria went on to a fruitful career with over $525,000 in career earnings and numerous stake victories.

Pollard's Vision, named for Seabiscuit's jockey Red Pollard who lost vision in his right eye, earned over $1.4 million in his racing career in the early 2000s, despite losing sight in an eye due to a side-effect from mare reproductive loss syndrome. That syndrome, detected in Kentucky in 2001, caused mares to abort or produce foals with complications and came from a rare infestation of eastern tent caterpillars in the States.

And the Ontario-bred filly Hard Not to Love, born at David Anderson's Anderson Farms in St. Thomas, won the Grade 1 La Brea Stakes in 2018, among other races, despite losing her eye in an accident as a two-year-old.

Since horses have larger eyes than most mammals that are placed on either side of their head, their peripheral vision is outstanding. Even with just one good eye, a horse can still see a bit on the side that is impaired.

"A horse's acuity, depth perception, and visual content identification is much worse than yours," said Dr. Janet L. Jones, cognitive scientist, long-time equestrian, and author of *Horse Brain, Human Brain: The*

Neuroscience of Horsemanship. "He compensates for his visual weaknesses with excellent hearing and a fantastic sense of smell."

Thankfully, the remainder of Emma's Bullseye's colt's first year was uneventful, at least from a freakish injury standpoint. For Simpson, her most dreaded days of the year were to come: weaning day.

In autumn, foals are separated from their mares as they prepare to enter their yearling season on January 1st. It is usually a traumatic, albeit brief, adjustment for moms and their babies.

"Not my favourite time of year," said Simpson. "We have a field up at the top of our property, separated from the barn area, and that is where we take the mares. We do two at a time. Usually, the mares and foals will whinny and cry for each other, but not for too long."

Emma's Bullseye's colt was weaned October 1st. By that time, he was getting familiar with living with other foals, learning how to quietly enter the barn and the stall, and having his temperature taken on a regular schedule.

When it came time for Cordes' one-eyed colt to move on to the next phase of his life as a yearling, he was sent to the Aschingers to be raised on the Kentucky bluegrass. Simpson was confident that the colt had a great chance to be successful.

"He left a few days before Christmas 2017, for the Aschinger's farm," said Simpson. "That is where Larry likes his yearlings to grow up before they are introduced to the saddle."

Coincidentally, as Cordes' colt was headed to Kentucky, his sire, Dramedy, was being relocated from War Horse Place to stand at stud at River Oaks Farm in Sulphur, Oklahoma, the home state of the stallion's owner John James. James wanted Dramedy to have a chance to breed more mares, including many of his own, to boost his stallion career.

But in the summer of 2019, James passed away at the age of seventy-five, and reluctantly, his wife Darlene sold the stallion to a farm in Saudi Arabia owned by Abdulrahman Alaloosh.

The Aschingers were well aware that they were welcoming a one-eyed colt from Cordes to their Kentucky farm. "Vera and Mike did a wonderful job with the colt," said Dana. "They had told us what happened and we were confident that because it had happened so early in his life, he really wouldn't have known anything different."

For the first half of 2018, Emma's Bullseye's boy spent most of his days roughhousing with other yearlings in the lush paddocks of Kentucky. He grew more accustomed to having plenty of human interaction, from grooming to having his feet picked out and going in and out of a stall.

"You are careful about handling them on the blind side, that's all, really," said Dana. "You do a lot of talking to them, so they always know where you are. You do all the same things as you would with a horse with both eyes, except just with a bit more caution and care.

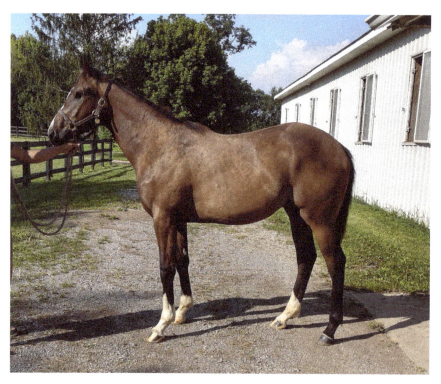

As a yearling, Mighty Heart was a good size and had good conformation. He just happened to be missing his left eye. Photo courtesy of Dana Aschinger.

"But I never thought he couldn't make it as a racehorse. He was beautiful, he had good bones, and was a well-balanced colt." Sadly, by the following spring, Dana's husband Gerry passed away and would not get a chance to follow along with the colt's journey to stardom.

In the fall of 2018, while many of his paddock mates were being prepared for yearling sales—to be sold by their commercial breeders in the hopes of a profit—the colt left War Horse Place to begin his early training with husband and wife team, Geoff and Sandra Mulcahy, at their Golden Vale Farm, twelve miles from War Horse Place. This is where the colt would be broken to saddle and bridle and ridden for the first time, arguably the most important stage of development for a young racehorse.

Factors such as pedigree, size, speed potential, and physical conformation are immensely important to a racehorse's success. Early nutrition, such as the exemplary program offered by Simpson, exercise, and conditioning are also integral.

But how a young horse is handled and taught his lessons as he begins his journey to the racetrack plays an important role in how a horse will approach his life as a racehorse. The Mulcahys, lifelong horsepeople from Ireland, were well respected in the business of early racehorse training.

"I got a call from Rachel Holden, the farm manager at War Horse Place, giving us the heads up that we were getting a one-eyed horse to break," said Geoff Mulcahy. "She said he was a bit timid but straightforward."

Mulcahy, who said he might have a one-eyed horse come around "maybe once every three years," was impressed with Emma's Bulleye's colt—his way of moving and his attitude.

"If a horse has a bad experience as a foal or even once he is already racing, it is usually forgotten about," said Mulcahy. "But if he has a bad experience in the breaking, they remember it and resent it.

They tend not to go forward in their training and get withdrawn. You must have patience and encourage them."

The breaking process begins with the tack: first the bridle and then the saddle. Many trainers of young horses will let a horse run (mostly bucking) around an arena when a saddle is first cinched up.

Weight on their backs is introduced with a rider lying across the horse and sitting atop while remaining in the stall.

Once the horse is used to the weight of the rider, he will be ridden in the arena or outside. This is where the horse learns steering, how to back up, and basic manners while listening to the rider's cues.

Because of his vision impairment, Cordes' colt took a little bit longer to be polished under tack. "We took things longer with him, about a couple of weeks," said Mulcahy. "Usually, breaking a horse is a five- or six-week process, but it was about seven weeks for him. He had to look at everything twice, but he learned his lessons very well."

On January 1st, the official birthday of all Thoroughbred racehorses, the Mulcahy-trained yearlings turned two years old and graduated to The Thoroughbred Center, a large training track close to the Mulcahy's farm where they educate the youngsters in a pseudo-racetrack setting.

This will get them used to a busier racetrack with more horses and noises, and they will learn to understand signals from riders as to when to speed up or slow down. Bones and muscles will slowly build strength with long, daily gallops before the youngsters are asked for any speed. In the spring of 2019, Emma's Bullseye's colt was ready to do a bit more.

"Larry came to visit him here in March, and we gave his colt a little speed work that day," said Mulcahy. "I tell you what, when it was time to send him to Josie at Woodbine, I told her, this one-eyed fellow can run a little bit."

Chapter 5:

Josie Carroll, the Trainer

JOSIE CARROLL WALKED DOWN the shedrow of her Woodbine barn and peeked into the first of sixty stalls. A grey-coloured filly was curled deep in her bedding, dozing, her ears occasionally flickering at the sounds of sparrows chirping.

"It's the quiet moments that we all cherish," she said. "The moments in the stall with the horses, feeling their breath on your cheek. This job has always been about the horses."

This moment is several hours removed from the hectic training time at the racetrack when a trainer and barn staff get busy preparing racehorses for the morning activities. From as early as 4:30 a.m., and for the next six hours, stalls are cleaned and freshly bedded, hay nets are stuffed with fresh flakes, horses are brushed and saddled for exercise. They are walked to cool out, given some grazing time on the lush grass, and then groomed, pampered, and fed. Some will be racing that day, which will stretch the work into the early evening.

There might even be a winner to celebrate, too.

Carroll often equates the job of a racehorse trainer to a coach of a sports team. A trainer has to know each horse intimately, plan an exercise regimen and feeding program that works for each horse, and map out races at the appropriate class level, distance and surface. Carroll has sixty horses owned by various Canadians and Americans in training at the track with some twenty-five staff members. Keeping owners informed and happy is also a big part of the job; after all, they are paying a daily rate of upwards of $90 per horse, plus vet and blacksmith bills. With smart phones and computers, it is hard for any trainer to have much time away from the job.

Carroll has sent out nearly nine hundred winners since she passed her trainer's test at Woodbine in 1994. She has not only prepared Canadian champions and millionaires, but her trainees have performed well south of the border. In 2019, she became the first woman trainer to be inducted into the Canadian Horse Racing Hall of Fame.

Like many young girls, Carroll was horse-crazy, period. Horses may be large and imposing animals, but their beauty and strength are an obsession for almost every young lady whether in the form of riding lessons, hours spent at a barn, or reading piles of horse books. Or all of the above.

Growing up in Toronto in the early 1970s, Carroll discovered Thoroughbred racing through the pages of the city's newspapers. "Every weekend, the newspapers had photos and stories about the stake races at Woodbine Racetrack," said Carroll. "I liked the racing game and would place pretend bets from the time I was very young. I would write down my picks from the race entries pages and check the results the next day. I wanted to know about the odds and how the sport worked."

But women on the racetrack in the late '60s and early '70s were a rarity. In fact, it was almost frowned upon. Male jockeys were known to boycott races if a recently-licensed woman was going to ride in the same race.

It was only 1969 when the first woman rode in a pari-mutuel race in the U.S.: Diane Crump broke the barrier and even rode in the Kentucky Derby the following year on her way to a successful career.

In a sport that is hundreds of years old, it was tough to find many women involved in horse racing. Usually, men would own and train the horses. On famous race days such as the Kentucky Derby or Queen's Plate, women donned their best fashion and watched as spectators.

In 1904, Laska Durnell was the first woman to own a Kentucky Derby starter, Elwood, who went on to win the race. Elwood was bought by Durnell's husband Charles but raced for his wife, who, as the legend goes, entered him in the Derby without her husband knowing. Elwood was also bred by a woman: Emma Holt Prather in Missouri.

Laska Darnell would not be able to race horses in her name much longer after the Derby win. Her Chicago stable was forced to disperse as she had broken a rule at the Chicago Jockey Club that forbade married women from making race entries in their own names.

Women owners became more commonplace at the Derby decades later, but women trainers in America's most famous race have been scarce. Since Mary Hirsch became the first woman to saddle a Derby starter in 1937, there have only been sixteen others, including Vickie Oliver, who started Hidden Stash in the 2021 edition. No woman trainer or jockey has won the Derby—yet.

Women appear a little more frequently in the history of Canadian racing, recorded to have established its roots in Quebec in 1767.

Mrs. Lily Livingston was influential in racing in Canada, as she brought well-bred horses to Ontario from the U.S. in the early 1900s. She did not live in Canada but had farms in Ontario and New Jersey. Her program challenged the top breeders in the province, and she pressured the OJC to alter its rules for entries to the King's (now Queen's) Plate, which stated that only if a British subject was residing in Ontario, were they allowed to enter a horse in the Plate.

Livingston was inducted into the Canadian Horse Racing Hall of Fame one hundred years later in the Thoroughbred Builder category.

Mildred A. Kane was the first woman owner to win a Queen's Plate when her bay colt Willie the Kid won the 1940 edition at old Woodbine Park. The Plate was already eighty years old at that point.

Yet, times have changed, and today women outnumber men in grooming and exercising horses on the backstretch of most racetracks in North America. Women are more plentiful in track management, online writing, and handicapping races.

Canada has had plenty of accomplished horsepeople who happen to be women.

Barbara Minshall, in 1996, became the first—and is currently the only—female trainer to be named Canada's Outstanding Trainer at the annual Sovereign Awards. No woman has won a Sovereign for Outstanding

Jockey, but Canada has produced top riders such as Joan Phipps, Francine Villeneuve, Chantal Sutherland, and Emma-Jayne Wilson who is the only woman to have ridden a Plate winner, doing so in 2007 aboard Mike Fox.

The Canadian Horse Racing Hall of Fame in 2020 and 2021 inducted two notable women 'builders' in the sport: Sue Leslie, the long-time president of the HBPA, the organization that provides benefits and services to owners and trainers; and Vicki Pappas, founder of the LongRun Thoroughbred Retirement Society, the first retired racehorse and adoption group of its kind in Canada, founded two decades ago.

"Gender has never come into play for me in this business," said Carroll. "People respect hard work and skills. I have a passion for it and I have never been afraid of work."

Much like Larry Cordes, Carroll has suffered great family loss. She was barely a year old when her mother, Elizabeth 'Lil' Carroll, passed away from cancer. Her father, Peter, was left with four children, Josie being all of just eighteen months old. A builder, Peter was developing subdivisions in their home city of Scarborough and needed help with his young family. It was their close family friend, 'aunt' Lotty Rinehart, who stepped in to essentially raise the youngest Carroll.

"It was a different era then," said Carroll, who was born on December 8, 1957. "There were four of us, and my dad was trying to get his building company off the ground.

I was fortunate to be raised by a strong, independent woman. Whatever I wanted to do, she had a quiet confidence in me and made it possible to follow my dream."

Carroll took riding lessons, and during her school years, enrolled in an equine studies program at the Humber College Institute of Technology and Advanced Learning less than a furlong from Woodbine Racetrack. Once her studies were complete, the college placed her in a job with veterinarian Dr. Darryl Bonder, where she assisted in surgeries.

Training racehorses was not yet on her radar until she got her first job in a racing stable, grooming horses for the very successful John Tammaro. Tammaro not only managed well-bred horses for the powerful Kinghaven Farms of 'Bud' Willmot, but also had a knack for claiming horses and developing them into stakes runners. Carroll graduated to assistant trainer under Tammaro's wing and spent several years in the U.S. with his American runners.

In the 1980s, when returning to Canada for her sister's wedding, Carroll spent her free time walking hots and met Mike Doyle, Canada's champion trainer in 1984, who offered her an assistant's job.

For more than a decade, Carroll was instrumental in assisting with the personable Irishman's top-notch operation. One of his horses, Wild Gale, owned by Little Fish Stable, provided Carroll with her first magical moment in racing—the Kentucky Derby walkover.

In 1993, Carroll accompanied Wild Gale from the barn to the saddling area for the one hundred nineteenth Derby. Despite being dismissed by the professional handicappers and scribes, Wild Gale ran furiously through the stretch as a longshot to be third to Sea Hero. He may have been a lot closer than the 2 1/2 lengths he lost by, had he not got into some traffic trouble in the stretch run. It was a moment, Carroll said, that brought tears to her eyes.

One year later, Doyle was hired by auto parts magnate and notable Canadian owner and breeder Frank Stronach to manage his stable. Carroll was ready to go out on her own, so Doyle recommended Carroll to his horse-owning clients such as Stronach and Thor Eaton, whose family owned the famous department stores, Eatons.

"Mike helped me immensely," said Carroll. "I had twenty horses to train right off the bat, but I needed capital. It was going to be about sixty days before horses started racing and money would be coming in. Mike introduced me to his bank manager, and I got a line of credit based on the accounts receivable of the clients he had turned over to me. That was the only way I was going to be able to do it."

A filly with the pretty name of Lilac Charm, owned by Stronach, was the first winner saddled by Carroll, her twenty-seventh starter in her first year of training in 1994. She has the official track-winning photo, the first of the almost nine hundred win photos she has stacked away today.

The following spring, her first stakes winner came when Tethra, owned by Eaton, won the Woodstock Stakes. She was on her way to a big career. Her stable expanded in quantity and also improved in quality. By 2001, her horses were earning over $1 million per season and would go as high as $3.5 million, averaging $2 million over the next twenty years.

Then along came two horses, both purchased at the Woodbine yearling sale by husband and wife teams from western Canada that would etch Carroll's name in horse racing history.

Edenwold, owned by Jim and Alice Sapara of Edmonton, Alberta, came into the 2006 Queen's Plate as a 16-to-1 longshot but came out the winner by three-quarters of a length to make Carroll the first woman to train a Plate winner. It landed her on the front page of the *Toronto Star* with the headline "TO Trainer Finally Gets Big Win on her Plate."

Getting the speedy Edenwold, the previous year's champion two-year-old colt, to stretch his early energy out to win the 1 1/4-mile Plate was no small feat. The chestnut colt, bred by small-scale breeders Gail Wood, Bill Diamant, and Vicki Pappas, had won three sprint stakes races as a two-year-old, and Carroll spent the spring of his sophomore year trying to slow him down. When his pre-Plate race saw him finish well in the Plate Trial at 1 1/8 miles, Carroll was confident. The Saparas were only in their sixth year of owning racehorses and already had a Plate win.

That first Plate victory remains vivid in Carroll's memory. "I remember when Edenwold came back after the race in front of the crowd, and you heard the roar of applause, people appreciating the horse that I had the privilege of training."

Edenwold was transformed from a short distance speedster as a two-year-old to a Queen's Plate champion in 2006 by trainer Josie Carroll. Photo by Terence Dulay.

From a historical standpoint, becoming the first woman to train a Plate winner was not lost on Carroll. "I appreciated that fact, but I was in competition with all other trainers, not just women trainers, trying to prepare our horse to do his best."

Five years later, Carroll was blessed with a big bay filly named Inglorious, owned by Vern and Donna Dubinsky from Sherwood Park, Alberta.

The Dubinskys, a young, fun-loving couple, had been breeding and racing horses on a small scale in Alberta and were having success. They stepped out and spent a bit more money on horses to race in Ontario, hired Carroll in the early 2000s, and soared to the top of the owners' list. In 2009, a $40,000 (USD) purchase, Careless Jewel, a headstrong but brilliantly quick filly, went from Woodbine to the legendary Saratoga racetrack and won the prestigious Alabama Stakes, a Grade 1 race, over the best fillies in America. Careless Jewel earned $1 million and was sold by the Dubinskys as a broodmare for $1.95 million.

Inglorious, a $90,000 (CAD) purchase at the Woodbine yearling sale, trounced colts in the Plate and was sold upon retirement for $1.35 million. The Dubinskys were voted Outstanding Owners of 2011 in Canada at the annual Sovereign Awards.

Carroll has maintained her place as one of the leading trainers in Canada, which she attributes, in her humble manner, to "good horses and good people." When you win races, people notice, and horses trained by Carroll are noticed throughout the continent.

Some of her dedicated staff have been with her for twenty years or more. She takes pride in teaching young barn staff who work their way up from hotwalker to groom, passing on her knowledge of horses and the importance of details.

"She sees things in horses that a lot of other trainers do not," said Lorie Allen, Carroll's long-time assistant trainer, who recently retired, but is still involved on big racing days and doing 'bookwork' for the trainer.

"When she takes that first walk through the barn in the morning, she is looking closely at every horse: how did they eat, how are they standing, are they chewing on things, do their teeth need to be done, how is their bedding, are they digging? Every detail has to be addressed."

Glenn Sikura, whose father John founded the successful Hill 'n' Dale Farm in Aurora, Ontario, has had horses with Carroll for three decades. His brother John Sikura Jr., who owns the massive Kentucky division of Hill 'n' Dale, has also been instrumental in sending Carroll impeccably bred horses. Champions Curlin's Voyage and Moonlit Promise are among those.

"Josie is a true horseperson," said Glenn Sikura. "Her success comes from her attention to her horses. She does not have to be a salesperson or a socialite. She spends her time with the horses. She is always available to her owners to talk, and she is open-minded when it comes to decisions on the horses."

One of the most important people in Carroll's life is her partner Charlie Nash, a respected horseman who has exercised the barn's runners and been integral in the stable's success. They have been together twenty-seven years.

"This is a really stressful business, and it is so important to have someone in your corner to keep you sane. Charlie is always positive, and that helps me. He helps me focus on what we do and what we can accomplish."

Josie Carroll was presented her Canadian Horse Racing Hall of Fame ring by mentor Mike Doyle. Photo by Clive Cohen/New Image Media/Canadian Horse Racing Hall of Fame.

When Carroll saw Mighty Heart for the first time in the spring of 2019, she could not remember working with many one-eyed horses and had never trained a horse with that handicap. She would soon discover the colt's quirks and phobias, and a new horse project is always an exciting challenge for Carroll.

"I was raised to believe you could do anything you want to do. From horses, I have learned to be patient, to study each individual, to find out what works best for each horse that will help him realize his full potential."

That mantra was shared by so many people who came together to form the Mighty Heart team.

Chapter 6:

Mighty Heart

IT IS A STRONG, beautiful, and appropriate name for a racehorse with a physical handicap and a horse owned by a family man. The name came easily to Cordes, and not only for those reasons. The original Mighty Heart, you see, is a cat.

Thoroughbreds can be named for free by submitting ideas to The Jockey Club in Kentucky before early February of their two-year-old year. The Jockey Club maintains a database of hundreds of thousands of the most sentimental, noble, clever, and even downright strange monikers. Famous horses such as Northern Dancer and Secretariat have their names 'retired' and thus cannot be used again.

Horse owners will often use the sire and dam to come up with a name. Dance Smartly was one of the greatest Canadian bred fillies in history and was named by Ernie Samuel's wife Elizabeth, who had a knack for creating beautiful horse names from the breeding. Dance Smartly's sire was Danzig (a son of Northern Dancer) and her dam was the champion mare Classy 'n Smart.

The great Secretariat, American Triple Crown winner in 1973, was a son of Bold Ruler. Seabiscuit, the rags to riches Thoroughbred from the 1940s, and the subject of a famous book and movie, was named from his sire Hard Tack, another name for the crackers eaten by sailors.

Or some may honour a person through the horse's name. In Canadian racing, many racehorses are named for hockey players, such as the 2020 champion two-year-old colt Gretzky the Great. Other names come straight out of the news. In 2019, a very fast four-year-old filly by the name of Covfefe became the year's Champion Female Sprinter in the U.S. Her name came from a viral meme, which came to life when President Donald Trump wrote the word in a late-night tweet, apparently misspelling the word 'coverage.' There are downright awful names too like Hoof Hearted (say it quickly), Go Ted, and Ham Sandwich.

Cordes loves telling the story of the original Mighty Heart, the Sphynx cat who became the best buddy of Cordes when he lived with his partner, Kimberley Rutschmann, in Port Perry.

Rutschmann's hobby was breeding the unusual hairless cats noted for their large ears and pointed faces, as well as their affectionate nature.

"You have to hear this story about this cat; it is a heart-wrenching story," started Cordes. "When this cat was born, he was the runt of the litter, half the size of the other kittens, and the mother cat kept taking the poor thing out and removing it from the others."

Rutschmann took over raising the kitten, feeding him with an eye-dropper for twelve weeks. But one day, the kitten stopped breathing, and Rutschmann had to resuscitate him.

That was only the first of many lives the little cat used up.

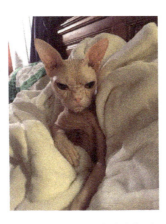

The original Mighty Heart, a Sphynx cat who eluded death numerous times, owned by Cordes' friend Kim Rutschmann. Photo courtesy Kim Rutschmann.

"Then, somehow, the cat gets outside when a door was left open, and it was winter," said Cordes. "He was essentially frozen, and Kimberley brought him back to life again. Then, when he was four years old, he had a stroke, and he couldn't sit up or stand, but he recovered from that, too."

The cat, which they had named Mighty Heart for his will to live, later had a large abscess in his stomach that they had to treat, eventually shrinking it with antibiotics.

"It's unbelievable what this cat has gone through," said Cordes. "He should have been dead from day one. We had named him Mighty Heart because he had to have a mighty heart to survive. So now, here is this racehorse I have, born in 2017. He loses an eye and now has his own major handicap. I just had to name him Mighty Heart."

It was impossible to know if the newly-christened Mighty Heart would be able to overcome a missing eye and be a winner on the track. But Josie Carroll and her dedicated staff were the right people to give him every chance to succeed.

As a two-year-old in the early summer of 2019, Mighty Heart was patiently brought along in his training. With the foundation of training he had in Kentucky with the Mulcahys, the colt was asked for speed in a workout each week, starting at short distances of two furlongs and gradually stretching out to half a mile.

In June of 2019, the Carroll barn was rolling along and preparing Ivan Dalos's colt Avie's Flatter for his quest for the Queen's Plate. Avie's Flatter had been named the Canadian Champion Two-Year-Old of 2018 based on his victories in the two biggest races for young horses, the Coronation Futurity and Cup and Saucer Stakes. He was the second favourite on Plate day and finished a gallant second to the front-running One Bad Boy, a Canadian-bred invader from California.

Just before the 2019 Plate, Mighty Heart was taken out of serious training. Carroll had detected some heat in the colt's left hind ankle, suggesting there was some inflammation. Not wanting to push the young horse, she told Cordes, and they agreed to send him back to Ballycroy Training Centre for some time off.

This attention to detail and care for the horse is what attracted Cordes to hiring Carroll late in 2016. "I was looking at a lot of different trainers at

Woodbine, their statistics with how many horses they started, victories and placings," said Cordes. "Josie had an excellent percentage of horses racing and doing well, and, at the same time, not being over-raced. I liked that."

Cordes had just two horses racing in the early part of 2019, both siblings of Mighty Heart. Touch of Emma had already won three races for Cordes and some $70,000 in Canadian coin, but she was claimed by another owner from a race in June. In Memory of Floyd was showing great promise in his first few races as a three-year-old, placing second four times before a big win in November, pushing his earnings to $100,000.

Mighty Heart, his ankle healed, had started getting serious in his training once again, and he was one of a dozen Carroll trainees sent to Fair Grounds racetrack in New Orleans in December when the Woodbine season ended. Carroll had another string of horses at Palm Meadows Training Centre near Boynton Beach, Florida, and entrusted her Fair Grounds horses to assistant Michael Lewars, a twenty-seven-year veteran from Woodbine.

It didn't take long for Lewars to find out he would have his hands full with Cordes' one-eyed colt.

"He was a little shifty at first, moving around a lot in the stall because of having just the one eye," said Lewars, who was born in Jamaica. "The groom who was supposed to look after him was a bit nervous about grooming him, so I ended up taking care of him."

Lewars had only worked with one other vision-impaired racehorse in his career, a gelding with the fitting name of Eye for an Eye, and he knew it would take a lot of patience and extra hours to get Mighty Heart comfortable with track routine.

"I had to play my way all around him, touch him on his blind side and let him know I was there. You had to worry if he was going to come right off the wall with all that shifting."

There were occasions when the colt did get himself in a tizzy. He banged his nose hard enough that he still has the bump and a scar to show for it.

Lewars also had to hand-walk Mighty Heart out for his gate schooling. "He was a little scared of the gate, so I just took him there with the rider, and we would walk him in and out of the gate to let him know he was all right. It was a matter of making him comfortable."

Before Mighty Heart's first race in February 2020, Lewars also took the colt from the barn to the saddling area on the front side of the Fair Grounds track half a dozen times to prepare for race day. "I really thought he could be any kind of horse. His bloodline was good, and he was a great mover. It was just a matter of us learning with him."

Carroll, always quick to give credit to her staff, praised Lewars's work with the colt as he neared his first career race.

"The work that Michael did with Mighty Heart in New Orleans was so important," said Carroll. "He put in so much time with him, and that was invaluable to the colt's development."

***

First career race
February 21, 2020
Fair Grounds, New Orleans
Maiden Special Weight, Purse $40,000, One Mile, Dirt

Results chart write-up from Equibase:

"Mighty Heart bumped with a rival at the start then bumped with another shortly thereafter and was taken up, lugged out badly into the first turn, went six then five wide on that bend, settled towards the rear, was ridden along while moving from two to four wide on the far turn, came five wide in the stretch under a drive and lacked the needed response."

The first career race for newly-turned three-year-old Mighty Heart was scheduled to be a grass race, but recent rains in the New Orleans area moved the event to the main track for safety reasons. He was a 12-to-1 longshot in the field of six horses who were all seeking their first career win.

Things started off awkwardly for Mighty Heart as he broke from post position two, but he was jostled about by rival horses to his inside and outside. The colt then made a beeline to the far outside of the track as his racing mates professionally headed towards the first turn.

"[For] the first part of the race, it looked like we were in a lot of trouble," said Carroll. "When the dirt flew back and hit him, he bolted to the outside of the track. The rider, Colby Hernandez, did a great job of pulling him back in with the field, and he actually finished up well."

Mighty Heart finished fourth, six-and-three-quarter lengths behind the winner, Dack Janiels.

"I always thought this horse could run, and he had schooled behind horses in [workouts] in the mornings," said Carroll. "But workouts are certainly not the same as a race."

Cordes was encouraged by his colt's finishing punch in the stretch run. "He really closed some ground at the end there, so that was good."

March 21, 2020
Fair Grounds, New Orleans
Maiden Special Weight, Purse $50,000, One Mile, Turf

Results chart write up from Equibase:

"MIGHTY HEART lugged out early, bore out badly on the first turn, settled inside of a rival, was roused while four-wide on the far turn and failed to respond."

Mighty Heart was so far back at the outset of his second career, a one-mile grass race, that track announcer John Dooley never said Mighty Heart's name during the entire running. The colt came out of his post position eleven in the fourteen-horse field in an awkward fashion and, once again, was headed straight for the parking lot as the first turn of the race came up quickly. It was all jockey James Graham could do to wrangle the colt back and inwards towards the rest of the field, but he was so far back that Dooley never even saw him.

You could almost hear Cordes' hand slap his forehead. He called Carroll after the race and wanted to know, was there was any point in continuing to try and race the colt?

Carroll was not ready to give up. "He had changed surfaces, and I thought he got a little panicked early in the race and, well, he was completely all over the place that day.

"I still had confidence in him, I am not sure why. I just thought that the talent was there, he just had some quirks. This is what trainers do; you have to find a way to figure them out and help them overcome all these things."

Later, it was discovered that Mighty Heart had a wolf tooth—one of several small, peg-like teeth in the cheek area that horses are born with but don't need—causing irritation with the bit in his mouth.

"Those first two starts, well, it was a combination of a lot of little things," said Carroll. "It was his inexperience and his racing erratically and the tooth. Actually, [it was hard for the dentist to get] the tooth out."

Cordes, who watched the colt's second race on Woodbine's expansive horse racing channel, Horseplayer Interactive, from Angela's Uxbridge home, was not completely convinced about the colt's future.

"He did the same thing in the second race as he did in the first race. I thought maybe the jockey might have been afraid of him; he left him out running in the middle of the track. Anyway, we quit on him at that point and brought him back to Canada. Josie kept saying to me, 'Larry, this is a nice horse,' so I went with that."

***

If there was one thing that Larry Cordes had learned about horse racing in forty years is that it can be a long waiting game for a winning horse. And anything and everything can happen.

Mighty Heart, following those two wonky races in New Orleans, was on his way back to Canada. His older half-brother, In Memory of Floyd, was unfortunately not going to make it back to the races, as his delicate physique was not going to hold up. Instead, Floyd joined Cordes' granddaughters Jennifer and Megan, who transitioned the family's favourite horse into a riding companion for their grandfather.

As 2020 dawned, Cordes had his small racing stable made up of Mighty Heart and a couple of two-year-olds including Evelyn's Delight, named for Larry's late daughter. Evelyn's Delight was also produced from his prized mare Emma's Bullseye. The three previous years for Cordes's racing stable showed purse winnings of an average of $40,000 per year from four wins, so his racing hobby was proving to be costly.

For each horse that Cordes had in training with Carroll, who charges about $100 per day, there are blacksmith bills, vitamins and supplements, veterinarian and chiropractic bills—all of which can total in the range of $4,000 per month.

"If you get lucky and win with your horse, there are the fees: ten percent to the trainer and jockey and one percent to the groom. Sometimes, after you pay all the bills, you end up with not much left."

In racing, any year you begin with lightly-raced young horses, hope springs eternal. But with the spring of 2020 came not only the threat of COVID-19, but another blow for Cordes.

Emma's Bullseye, who was back at Vera Simpson's Curraghmore Farm, had just foaled another filly. This filly was by the young stallion Ami's Holiday, who had won the 2014 Breeders' Stakes, the third jewel of Canada's Triple Crown and earned almost $1 million. Immediately after foaling, however, Emma's Bullseye began to show signs of colic. This gastrointestinal condition causes abdominal pain and can occur from excess gas, an obstruction, or twist in the intestines. It is the number-one cause of premature death in horses.

Emma's Bullseye was rushed to the Ontario Veterinary College at the University of Guelph, where Mighty Heart had his eye removed, and it was determined surgery was needed: the foal's birth had caused a twist in her intestines. The mare was in great pain and was given medication and prepped for surgery, but she died before the operation.

"It was a tremendous loss," said Cordes. "The foal, she was just gorgeous, and she was put on a nurse mare. But it was devastating."

And then, the COVID-19 pandemic put a stop to the world, causing death and sickness and fear. Businesses were shut down. Horse races were put on hold for two months. By the time the first wave of the virus began to dissipate and the summer brought the opening of the economy, Cordes's stable got even smaller.

His two-year-olds were returned to Ballycroy Training Centre to grow and mature; one of them, Trigger's Bay, from his mare Trigger Finger, had hurt his ankle in his first race and had to have minor surgery.

"That left me with just one horse who was racing, Mighty Heart. At that point, I almost said, 'To heck with this business.' It was just getting frustrating again."

Ah, but there was Mighty Heart, who would start to show the talent that Josie Carroll knew was there. Cordes's racing luck was about to turn around.

Chapter 7:

The Team

SIOBHAN BROWN FELT AN immediate connection with the one-eyed Mighty Heart when she first saw him in 2019. The colt, young and still very raw from a polished racehorse standpoint, was in the care of another groom, and the thirty-two-year-old Brown was just starting her third year as a racehorse groom and second year with Josie Carroll. She, too, was still learning the ropes of her profession. Like Mighty Heart, she had to overcome the many hurdles that life can throw at one person: a diagnosis of epilepsy as a teenager, the loss of a special person in her life, and then a 2,100-kilometre journey away from the only home she had ever known.

Fate surely had a hand in bringing her together with Cordes' quirky colt.

Groves Point, Nova Scotia, is a dot of a community on the northeastern tip of the province in the municipality of Cape Breton, with a provincial park and pebbly beaches on the waters of Bras d'Or Lake. There are only around six hundred people living in the area where Brown was born and raised.

Brown, the only child of Gwen Boyce and Tom Brown, was an energetic, sporty, animal-loving youngster with lofty dreams. She had a talent for gymnastics, which she pursued in earnest while attending Holy Angels High School, the only publicly-funded all-girls school east of Montreal.

She was a cheerleader and, after graduation, pondered jobs with the RCMP or driving a long-haul truck cross-country.

She loved horses, too, but only ever saw them at nearby riding stables or occasionally at Truro Raceway, a Standardbred track that was a three-hour drive to the west, when she visited her mother's parents who lived close to that track.

But Brown's world came crashing to a halt in 2005 in the courtyard of Le Louvre Museum in Paris, France.

"We had just arrived in Paris for a school trip," said Brown. "I had been stressing about the flying, excited about trip so I didn't sleep for twenty-four hours."

She had her first seizure while visiting Le Louvre and was rushed to the hospital. Doctors soon let her return to the hotel, where she had another seizure. She spent three days in the hospital, and it was believed that her seizures were epileptic.

"I never did see the Eiffel Tower," laughed Brown.

She can laugh sixteen years later, but at the time, her world flipped over. Once back in Nova Scotia, doctors confirmed she had epilepsy, a disorder of brain activity that can cause unpredictable seizures. For two out of three people who have epilepsy, the cause is unknown. That was the case with Brown.

"It was horrendous," said Boyce, a retired schoolteacher. "I had to remove her from gymnastics and cheer-leading. She lost her driver's license and had to give up a lot of her favourite things."

As doctors tried to get Brown on the correct medication, she fell, losing consciousness during a seizure that she didn't feel coming on, and broke an ankle.

"We figured out some of the triggers for my seizures—stress, lack of sleep, and low blood sugar—but there weren't any clues as to when they would come on," she said.

One of her last seizures, about a decade ago in the Sydney hospital, was so serious "it almost killed me, it was terrifying." Finally, she responded to a drug called Keppra and slowly returned to a somewhat normal life.

It wasn't easy.

"She lived in such a dark fog on her medication; she could hardly learn in school after that," said Boyce. "We later found out that the drug caused learning disabilities."

Graduating from high school was difficult, but Brown was resilient. She set out to find her way in the working world and had enjoyed working at a local riding stable and animal rescue farm. It was at the rescue farm, Rocking Horse Ranch, where she met a six-month-old filly foal who began following her around. When Brown found out the filly had been born on her birthday, she bought her. She still has Summer today.

Siobhan Brown has owned Summer since she was a foal. Photo by John Ratchford.

But Brown was seeking a career and with a chance of seizures, albeit minimal, on her profile, finding such a path proved difficult. Truck driving jobs were off the table, and the RCMP wanted her to have more 'life experience,' so Brown took a job at Tim Horton's. "Really, a lot of people don't ever leave the island. In Cape Breton, you either get work at restaurants or call centres."

During her time at Tim Horton's, one of Brown's most cherished family members, her great aunt Helen McNeill, passed away at the age of eighty-nine. "She was a spitfire, and she taught me strength and how to stand up for myself. I wanted to go to her funeral in Truro, but my job wouldn't give me the time off."

Brown went anyway, returned home, and left her Tim Horton's job. "It was like my aunt Helen was guiding me. It turned out to be the best thing I ever did."

Soon after, she saw a Facebook post by fellow Cape Bretoner, Tyler Clark, who had moved to Ontario to work with racehorses at Woodbine racetrack. The post said there were jobs available at the track. Brown packed up her car and headed east.

"I said, 'What the heck are you doing?' I didn't want her to go," said Boyce. "But she's a tough kid and very strong-willed. The epilepsy had been under control for five years, and she said she wanted to go and try it."

Brown drove through Maine and New York to Niagara Falls and arrived in Ontario in the summer of 2016. "I knew it was going to be a long time not seeing my family, but if you worry about something months down the road, you miss things in between. I wanted to focus on right here and right now."

Brown moved into the track dormitory and started working as a groom for one of the leading trainers at Woodbine, Malcolm Pierce, and his wife and assistant Sally. The Pierces and their staff brought her along slowly, teaching her the racetrack routine and horse-care skills, but at first, it was overwhelming for Brown, and she moved down a job level and became a hotwalker.

"I cried almost daily out of frustration and stress trying to adjust to the track life," said Brown. "Early on, I realized I wasn't ready to be a groom just yet, and it was something I was going to have to work really hard for."

After returning home for the winter, she went back to Woodbine in 2017 and was ready to take on the groom's job again. The next year, she joined Carroll's barn when the Pierces began to downsize.

Her biggest moment came in October 2018, when she led over Ivan Dalos's three-year-old filly Lonhro'scollection for a race, and she won. Carroll had the official win photograph of the race labelled 'Groom Siobhan Brown Captures First Lifetime Win.' It was an emotional moment for Brown. "It brought back my memories of my aunt Helen, how her passing gave me the courage and strength to stand up for myself and do what I believe is best for me. My goal for 2018 was to bring a horse into the winner's circle. Two-and-a-half years after I just up and left Nova Scotia, here I was."

Another first for Brown was going to Florida with the Carroll stable for the winter, where most of the horses have time off before returning to Ontario for the following season.

The racetrack life, the long hours and physical work was a big adjustment for Brown. Would she stick it out? She did, and soon she would meet the horse that would change her life.

***

Jennifer Perrin was only four years old when her father, Jim, passed away of osteogenic sarcoma, the same bone cancer that felled the famous Terry Fox.

Her mother, Angela, had just lost her mom, Connie, and in a couple of years, Jennifer would say goodbye to aunt Evelyn, Angela's sister.

She remembers a little about her dad; he loved a different kind of horse-power: motorcycles, dirt bikes, and "anything with a motor," said Jennifer. "But he did grow up on a horse farm, and some of his family had horses, so he enjoyed our interest in horses."

Neither Jennifer nor Megan remember their 'nana' Connie, but many agree Jennifer has a strong resemblance to the family matriarch. It was a lot of sadness for the young Perrin children to bear, but as young adults, they grew to be positive and respectful, learning from their grandfather and mother that nothing can be taken for granted.

Like their mother, Angela, the Perrin girls are horse-crazy and have always been involved in riding and training young horses for the show ring. The two girls became accomplished equestrians on the hunter circuit. Megan was well advanced on Ontario's jumper 'A' show circuit before suffering from a concussion in early 2020 that curtailed any professional riding. All three women have enjoyed working with young, inexperienced horses and retired racehorses. Their brother Tom, who does not live with his sisters, has not followed the horses closely but Angela's brother Darin and his son and daughter Kyle and Toni are keen followers of their grand-father's horses.

But it is Jennifer and her mother who are the most involved with Larry's Thoroughbreds, and Perrin took a much bigger role with the stable at Woodbine in the spring of 2019 through her interest in magnetic therapy.

Her own sport horses were enjoying the benefits of Pulsed Electromagnetic Field therapy (PEMF), and she suggested to her grandfather that he try it on his racehorses.

Megan Perrin is an accomplished showjumper. Here she is on Graffiti.
Photo by Andrew Ryback.

Magnetic therapy has been used on humans and animals for two thousand years. Molecules in the body have natural magnetic energy, which can, at times, become unbalanced. The premise of magnetic therapy is that a magnetic field presented near the body will adjust and stimulate the magnetic energy. Pulsed magnetic therapy uses coils that are placed on various parts of a human's or animal's body. It is said to boost metabolism, aid in overall health, and soothe muscle soreness, and in humans, it is used in assisting with depression. It is non-invasive, non-medicinal, and human clients rave about the therapy for aches and pains.

Perrin began working on In Memory of Floyd, the older half-brother of Mighty Heart, when he was beginning his career in 2019. Cordes was impressed.

"This treatment is an amazing thing," said Cordes. "I got her to start using it on all my horses, and I swear by it. It does wonders for their muscles."

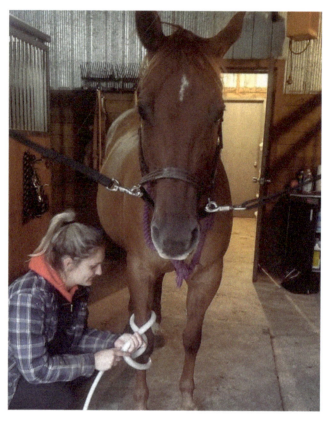

Jennifer Perrin bought her own PEMF machine and treats horses at farms and at Woodbine. Photo courtesy of the Cordes' family.

Perrin, wanting to build up a career working with racehorses, ended up purchasing her own PEMF system with her savings. "Well, it was either buy a house or buy the machine," laughed Perrin. "I bought the machine."

Perrin's business expanded so much that by 2020 she had dozens of clients at the racetrack and others in the equestrian circles. Like Brown, Perrin would soon be front and centre with Mighty Heart when he embarked on his magical racing year.

***

While Brown and Perrin were relatively new to the world of the backstretch barn area at the racetrack, Des McMahon grew up at the track. His father, Bill, was a journeyman jockey at Woodbine in the '70s, '80s, and '90s and rode in a number of Queen's Plates. The younger McMahon, who grew up in Tottenham, Ontario, worked his summer jobs 'on the ground' at the track, but it wasn't until he was in his twenties when he climbed aboard and began exercising horses.

"I had really bad asthma as a kid that I had to overcome," said McMahon. "I never let it deter me, though, from working with the horses."

McMahon moved to Fort Erie and close to that town's racetrack, where he galloped horses and started a family. Job offers came in from Woodbine, including winter work in Florida with Carroll, and McMahon has been commuting the two hours north to Rexdale weekly from his home ever since.

He joined Carroll's Woodbine team in 2018 and got an afternoon job working in the silks room (organizing each day's owner's colours that the jockeys wear in each race). Doing double duty at Woodbine on race days means McMahon leaves his family in Fort Erie for four days every week and stays near the track to avoid the long commute. "Being away from them is tough, but we do a lot of chatting on Facetime."

A good exercise rider is quiet, with light hands and the ability to keep a horse fit and happy. In this role, McMahon is tasked with taking his daily mounts out for exercise with instructions from Carroll. This can involve lightly jogging his horses or 1 1/2-mile gallops around the Woodbine track, plus long walks to and from the track.

His first ride on Mighty Heart came when the colt arrived from the Mulcahys in Kentucky in 2019.

"He was like a normal baby," said McMahon, "Although, with only one eye, he had to look at things a bit longer to get used to them. He was a colt, and sometimes they can be studdish and tough to handle, but he was never a bad actor, and through that first year training at Woodbine, we all thought he had a bit of talent."

***

The formation of Mighty Heart's team even had beginnings in East Asia and Africa, with two young men from two islands 10,000 kilometres apart who fatefully met at Woodbine.

On the other side of the world, horse racing in Japan is a far more popular and recognized sport than in Canada and North America. Close to $30 billion is wagered on racing each year—more than twice what is bet on racing in North America. Racing and breeding are high-scale in Japan, with many large breeding farms importing horses from the U.S. to race or stand at stud. Racing and equestrian sports are so woven into the fabric of Japanese life that its schools incorporate jockey instruction into their curriculum.

Daisuke (Canadian pronunciation is *dice-kay*) Fukumoto grew up on a small farm in the rolling countryside of the small island of Kagoshima at the southernmost tip of Japan. His father worked in the racing industry for a few years, grooming at Saga racetrack, while the young Fukumoto always had ponies around to ride. He learned the finer aspects of riding at a local stable for jumpers and then rode in pony races and other races for retired racehorses on bush tracks.

As a teenager, Daisuke entered the Japan Racing Academy, a very competitive and difficult process in which two hundred applicants take seven exams and only twenty aspiring riders advance. Fukumoto was not selected in the final cut, but that did not stop him from following his dream. He watched a lot of racing from North America and was impressed with the riding style in Canada and the U.S. in which jockeys sat a lot more still on horseback during a race. This differed from the much more active style of riders in Japan and Europe, who tend to move a lot on a horse to encourage them.

He was just seventeen years old and without much more than 'hello' as his knowledge of the English language when he hopped on a plane to Canada.

"My parents wanted me to try to ride in Japan, but I wanted to go to North America," said Fukumoto. "They didn't want me to go away, but I kept talking about it every day [and] they finally let me go."

One of the first things he did when he arrived in Canada was to enroll in English language classes before he set out to find work at the Woodbine

Racetrack. Coincidentally, the first day Fukumoto visited the track was Queen's Plate day in 2015.

"It was amazing," said Fukumoto. "I just knew that was where I wanted to be, riding in the Queen's Plate."

Des McMahon (left) exercises horses for Josie Carroll, including Mighty Heart, at right, shown with jockey Daisuke Fukumoto. Photo by Jeff Bowen.

One of the first trainers to give the young Japanese rider a chance to exercise horses was Reade Baker, who liked how the young man handled his horses and got them to relax. It was at Baker's barn where Fukumoto met Pram Seebah, who was grooming and walking horses for the Hall of Fame trainer.

Pram Seebah had been in Canada for four years when he met Fukumoto, having moved from his birthplace on the island of Mauritius off the southeastern coast of South Africa. Seebah was just four years old when he accompanied his grandfather to the races and was taught how to read the track program and racing information. It was not easy, however, to get a job in racing in his home country.

"Horse racing in Mauritius is a very niche thing," said Seebah. "Only relatives of trainers would get the best jobs in the industry, and sometimes it could take five years just to become a groom."

Seebah actually went to law school in England when he turned nineteen, but when his parents relocated to Canada in 2011, Seebah dropped out and went directly to Woodbine, where he began walking horses and grooming.

"I wanted to become a trainer. In Mauritius, there are only four or five trainers who train all the horses, and they are all very rich, but I learned it was not the same thing in Canada."

In fact, becoming a Thoroughbred trainer at Woodbine might not take nearly as long if you work your way up from groom to assistant trainer, pass the trainer's test, and then have horses for clients to train. You also need plenty of capital in the bank to start your own stable to pay staff and buy feed.

Seebah worked for a variety of different trainers—Mark Casse, a member of the Horse Racing Halls of Fame in Canada and the U.S., and Canadian Hall of Fame inductees Robert Tiller and Reade Baker—but it didn't look like he was going to become a trainer just yet.

When he met Fukumoto, the two young men hit it off, communicating about international horse racing, of which Seebah was a fan, despite the obvious language barrier.

"We became friends, and I helped him with his paperwork to be able to work and ride in Canada. At the same time, I suggested to him that I could be his agent at the track," said Seebah.

Most jockeys have an agent who lines up all the horses for the rider for each racing day; it is a job that involves knowing how to handicap a race and project upcoming winners. "I had been handicapping races almost all my life, and to be an agent, you have to watch all the races and figure out what horses will be pointed to what upcoming races and who can potentially win them. I was excited to try that."

Fukumoto and Pram set out for their first year as jockey and agent in 2017. Riding as a ten-pound apprentice (horses ridden by 'rookie' riders get weight allowances), Fukumoto rode his first Woodbine winner on his birthday, October 13, and as is tradition, was promptly hoisted up by fellow jockeys and dunked in water.

The following year, in his first full season as a jockey, and up one level to a five-pound apprentice, Fukumoto won thirty-six races against a competitive colony of riders that included multiple champion jockeys: Eurico Rosa da Silva; Patrick Husbands; Emma-Jayne Wilson; and another young rider from Japan, Kazushi Kimura. It was Kimura, also an apprentice, who attracted a bit more attention from the Woodbine horsepeople, and by year's end he had won over one hundred races and was named the year's top apprentice.

But Fukumoto continued to progress, winning fifty-two races in 2019, passing the million-dollar mark in purses as his horses collected $1.4 million.

"When he started, I was getting mixed feedback on his riding," said Seebah. "But he really improved a lot in his first couple of years, and our business started doing very well."

The two friends, who had to learn about their respective jobs quickly, were on a fast trajectory to racing history.

Chapter 8:

A Mighty Ride

SOFT BRUSH IN HAND, Siobhan Brown makes short strokes starting behind Mighty Heart's ears, down the colt's neck to his shoulder. Long passes of her brush begin at the horse's withers, down his back and his powerful hindquarters. It is just after 5:30 a.m., and Brown has already been at work at the Josie Carroll barn for over an hour. Brown likes to get an early start in getting the horses she grooms for trainer Josie Carroll ready for training, but 'Willie,' the nickname given to him by Jennifer and Brown's friend and fellow groom, Linda Davis, is still snoozing. Most days, Brown will just work around a prone Mighty Heart, cleaning his stall while he continues to nap.

Once Mighty Heart is up and ready to go, exercise rider Des McMahon puts on the colt's saddle and bridle and heads out to the track for the morning gallop. Brown grabs the colt's feed tub and water bucket for a quick rinse. The colt's stall will be fluffed up with fresh bedding of pine shavings and his hay net plumped with fresh fodder.

Brown has four other horses in her section and will repeat the process for everyone for the next few hours. The mornings are fast and furious as training hours are limited, usually ending at 10:30 a.m.

When Mighty Heart comes back into the barn after his energetic run around the track, Brown bathes him, and a hotwalker takes over and cools out the colt for about thirty minutes. The colt will then get some grazing time on the grass outside the barn before he heads back into his stall.

Bandages are wrapped with care around each leg to protect the delicate bones, tendons, and ligaments. A lunch of oats, salt, and vitamins is served to each horse by 11:00 a.m. The shedrow is raked and tidied before Brown goes home, coming back if it is her turn to feed dinner at 4:00 p.m. or if one of her horses is racing that afternoon.

The job of a groom can be gruelling, but they do it for their love of horses and the pride in preparing them to race—long hours of physical work for pay that amounts to not much more than $100 per day. Should one of a groom's horses get lucky and win a race, they will receive a small percentage of the winner's share and perhaps an extra bonus from a generous owner or jockey.

Brown took over the care of Mighty Heart when he came in from Ballycroy Training Centre at the onset of the COVID-19 pandemic in May 2020. It had been a nail-biting return to Ontario for Brown, who just got into the province as borders were being closed and businesses, including racing, were about to be put on hold.

Brown saw the colt's name on the list of horses due to arrive at Carroll's Woodbine barn and had developed a fondness for him the previous year when another Carroll employee was grooming him.

"My friend Linda was working in the same barn and always gave him a carrot when he walked by," said Brown. "I started doing the same thing to the point where he would stop outside my working area, stomp his foot and wait for his carrot. I think both Linda and I had a soft spot for him because he had just one eye, but he was just such a neat horse. We said to each other, 'Maybe he could be a good horse if he got lots of love.'"

When Brown found out that Mighty Heart's groom from 2019 was not returning for 2020, she approached Carroll and asked if she could groom Mighty Heart.

Carroll agreed, but Brown had to give up one of the five horses she was already grooming. She said goodbye to Kid's Mischief, the first horse she began looking after for Carroll, and ushered Mighty Heart into her life.

"The first thing I did was check the results of his races he had run in New Orleans. I saw a fourth-place finish and his second race where he finished eleventh, and I thought, 'Uh oh, what was I thinking?'"

Carroll gave Brown a little project to work on with Mighty Heart. The colt was not a fan of having his handlers lift his lip to show his tattoo number, which is needed for identification before each race.

"The first time I tried to do it, he pretty much picked me up off the ground and was throwing me around," said Brown. "I started using pieces of carrots to give to him while I played around with his lip. It was almost two months before he was better at allowing the horse identifier to check his tattoo, although he still doesn't like it."

The good news for Mighty Heart is like all Thoroughbreds born in 2017 or later, he has a tiny microchip implanted in his neck that is becoming the main process of horse identification. The chip can be scanned before a race to give information such as pedigree, date of birth, and markings.

Brown and Mighty Heart had started to build a special bond, and they gained confidence from each other. The colt also thrived under his morning rider McMahon, whose calm demeanour meshed well with the now three-year-old, who quickly showed signs that he wanted to do more.

"I noticed a big difference in him when he came back from Fair Grounds," said McMahon. "Suddenly, he was snorting and feeling strong when he went on to train. He was a lot more confident."

Mighty Heart certainly had filled out, with powerful hindquarters, a wide and muscular chest, and strong forearms. It was easy to see a physical resemblance to his great-great-great-grandfather, Northern Dancer.

While Carroll's barn of equine athletes was well underway with training, so were almost another thousand runners on the Woodbine backstretch. The trainer had made an important addition to her stable, assistant Suzanne Lorimer, a long-time assistant trainer to Roger Attfield and respected horsewoman.

But racing was still on hold a month after the scheduled mid-April start date of the season because of the pandemic. Instead of the excitement of entering horses in races and giving chances to their owners for some purse money, Carroll was spending hours on the phone with frustrated owners, speaking to media about how important the sport and industry was to the province, and trying to keep up the morale of her own staff. The big races of the year, such as the Queen's Plate and the Woodbine Oaks—the filly equivalent of the Plate—were pushed back for more than two months and mapping out races for her top runners to get to those big events was a guessing game.

Finally, in early June, racing had been given the green light to start, but the protocols for race days were strict: no fans were allowed to attend— something that had never happened in the two hundred fifty-year history of horse racing in Canada. Owners were also not permitted to watch their horse's race, and only the trainer and the groom were allowed inside the saddling enclosure with a runner. But racing was on, and that was good news.

While Carroll was picking out big-money stakes races for her stable stars, such as the 2019 Champion Two-Year-Old Filly Curlin's Voyage, an Oaks and Plate hopeful, she had other lightly-raced horses that were in the early stages of their careers. Mighty Heart was in this group, and she was pleased with his progress. The colt was training over Woodbine's Tapeta surface, much different from a traditional dirt track found at most tracks in North America. Tapeta, created by successful English trainer Michael Dickinson, is a mixture of silica sand, wax, and fibres that have been extensively researched and simulates the root structure of grass or turf. The surface is listed as an 'all-weather' track that does not retain water and can be used in all types of weather. It is also considered a much safer surface than many traditional dirt tracks, yielding a lower number of injuries to horses. All-weather tracks debuted in the late 1980s in England, where most of the races are on turf, a surface that cannot be used in inclement weather.

Woodbine was one of the first North American tracks to install an all-weather track; Polytrack replaced the dirt track in 2006 before the much more favourable Tapeta brand was installed in 2016. Today, there are about half a dozen tracks on the continent that use an all-weather surface. Woodbine also has a unique European-style turf course around the outside of the main track and had recently converted the inner Standardbred gravel track into another grass course.

As Mighty Heart's first race at Woodbine approached, he would have new equipment, too. There was some thought from Carroll's team that having his left-side, eyeless area exposed to the kickback of track surface might have been causing him some discomfort. A 'bubble' blinker was affixed to a hood that the colt would wear when he went to the post for the third time in his career.

July 11, 2020
Woodbine Racetrack
Maiden Special Weight, Purse $102,500, 1 1/16 miles, Tapeta surface

Race call from Woodbine track announcer Robert Geller:

"Locked up, and they're off . . . going for the lead are Artie My Boy, Fort Hope and on their hem, Mighty Heart . . . out in front in a stacked field, Fort Hope, Artie My Boy and three wide Mighty Heart . . . Artie My Boy in front, a neck away in second Fort Hope, one length to Mighty Heart . . .

"As they go into the turn, it's still Fort Hope and Artie My Boy together, Fort Hope just in front, one [length] to Mighty Heart. At the helm, still Artie My Boy and now at the leader's girth, Mighty Heart . . . down the lane and out wide Mighty Heart's got the lead . . . it's Mighty Heart, the Josie Carroll runner Mighty Heart with a big heart by four lengths."

It was hard to know what to expect from 'Willie' when he stepped onto the track for his first race as a three-year-old.

At 13-to-1 odds and a longshot against ten other sophomores also seeking their first win, Mighty Heart was very strong early on and dragged jockey Justin Stein to join the front runners before coming back to his rider and settling into a steady cadence. Stein moved his hands ever so slightly, giving the colt the signal to go, and they moved well wide of his rivals and out to the lead. He won by four-and-one-quarter lengths.

A collective sigh of relief and more than just a little bit of excitement came from Carroll and Brown.

"He had trained really, really well going into that first race at Woodbine," said Carroll. "And he had worked like a horse that was going to win a race. I was more apprehensive about how he was going to behave in the race, so we went into it with bated breath—would he run his race or pull another stunt?"

Siobhan Brown had to blink hard as the colt drew off from his flagging rivals in the deep stretch,. No, it wasn't a dream.

"It was a 'holy crap' moment for me," said Brown. "I know he had been training well, but I don't know if any one of us knew what to expect. To see him win like that, it was one of the most exciting moments for me since I got to the track."

In the winner's circle, Brown and assistant Lorimer gave Mighty Heart some affectionate rubs on his nose while Carroll gave the colt some good pats on his neck. Cordes, not permitted to be at the track due to pandemic protocols, watched from home, cheering and high-fiving his family.

It was two months to the Queen's Plate, and Carroll had watched Curlin's Voyage win her prep race for the Woodbine Oaks, the Fury Stakes, with a late flurry to win by a head. The filly was on track for the August 15th Oaks, and a good race there would put her in the Plate against the boys. Mighty Heart and another lightly-raced colt in the Carroll barn, Belichick, were also possible Plate starters but they had some proving to do first. Both colts were headed for races on August 1st.

August 1, 2020
Woodbine Racetrack
Allowance race, Purse $95,990 1 1/8 miles, Tapeta

Race call from Woodbine track announcer Robert Geller:

"Locked up . . . and they're off! And shooting across, very keen, is going to be Court Battle, going forward on the inside Desolator, they're up in front narrowly from Golden Wave. On the outside is Courtly Manner, they're going pretty fast. Over on the inside, just set-tling in behind them early on is Tecumseh's War with a nice position and then Mighty Heart . . .

"And still not an easy lead for Desolator, about a half in front, second place is Court Battle on the inside, Tecumseh's War, Courtly Manner the outside, about a length behind them over on the inside is Frankie Barone and racing on the outer, Mighty Heart.

"Court Battle and Courtly Manner in front at the top of the home stretch with Mighty Heart down the outside . . .

"Out in front narrowly Court Battle, on the inside kicking on is Tecumseh's War and flying home Timeskip right over the top of them all. Timeskip is flying home on the outside with Tecumseh's War, and Timeskip has got up to win, back in third place, Mighty Heart."

Twenty-one days after his first career win Mighty Heart stepped up one class from his maiden win to the allowance level. He was not only meeting other horses who had won races, but was facing older horses while stretching out to 1 1/8 miles for the first time.

It was a good effort from Mighty Heart, who had to give up some extra ground going wide into the stretch run. The winner, Timeskip, was a well-seasoned five-year-old who was winning for the fourth time in his career for trainer Renée Kierans. To the inside of Mighty Heart, at the finish, was fellow Plate hopeful Tecumseh's War, trained by Catherine Day Phillips.

"We rushed him back a bit for that allowance race," said Cordes. "He had a short lead until a sixteenth of a mile from the finish, and two horses just nipped him. Josie said to me, 'Okay, we know he's got talent, I am going to train him into the Plate.'"

Training the colt 'into the Plate' meant he would not have another race before the Plate and was the only move Carroll could make with the colt since trying to squeeze in another race between August 1st and the September 12th Plate would be too much, too soon in Mighty Heart's brief career. In fact, Carroll decided to use the same strategy with Belichick, a big, brawny colt owned by American stables LNJ Foxwoods and NK Racing. Belichick raced later that day, finishing second in a maiden race and would go to the Plate seeking his first career win.

Carroll's best chance at a third Plate victory seemingly lay with the agile filly Curlin's Voyage, who put in an impressive run to win the $500,000 Woodbine Oaks on August 15th, defeating the top Canadian-bred three-year-old fillies at 1 1/8 miles. Curlin's Voyage, who was ridden by multiple-time champion jockey Patrick Husbands, ran the distance in 1:50.04, faster than the 1:50.61 needed by Clayton to win the important Plate Trial Stakes earlier that day. Clayton had won the Trial by half a length in a testing stretch battle with Halo Again, a colt who had cost $600,000 as a yearling and was trained by Steve Asmussen, one of the world's winningest conditioners. Dotted Line, a plucky Ontario-bred gelding, was just a head back in third.

Fillies who beat the best of their set in the Oaks have done very well in the Plate. In the first one hundred sixty runnings of the race—known as the 'gallop for the guineas' —there have been thirty-seven fillies that have won. Since 2000, four Oaks' winners have come right back to win the Plate, including Carroll trainee Inglorious in 2011. Carroll had every reason to be confident in her chances to win another Plate with Curlin's Voyage while quietly having faith in her lightly-raced colts Mighty Heart and Belichick.

The Plate is the Stanley Cup for Thoroughbred racing's owners, trainers, jockeys, and breeders. It is older than the Stanley Cup, having its first edition in 1860, while the first Stanley Cup was presented to the Montreal Hockey Club in 1893. The Plate is older than *Canada* by seven years and is the longest continuously run horse race in North America. It is the date circled on the calendar of not only horse racing fans, but Toronto sports fans. Pre-Covid, it had morphed into a weekend festival and *the* must-attend social event of the summer.

It was the Toronto Turf Club in 1859 that requested Her Majesty Queen Victoria pledge a 'plate' trophy for the winner of the first running of the race, and she obliged with a 'Plate of Fifty Guineas.' Thus, the 'gallop for the guineas' was born.

From its first running at the Carleton Race Course in what is now the west end of Toronto, the Plate has attracted top horses, dignitaries, aristocrats, and the hoi polloi.

The qualifications to run a horse in the race were wildly different from the start: only horses from Upper Canada that had never won 'public money' were allowed in the early years. Since 1946, the race has been open to all Canadian-born three-year-old Thoroughbreds.

The race is now worth $1 million, and while plenty of royalty has visited Woodbine to take in the race, the last such visit was in 1997 when Her Majesty Queen Elizabeth and Prince Philip presented the Plate trophy to Dom Romeo for his gelding Big Red Mike.

The Plate also leads off the Canadian Triple Crown, which is completed by the Prince of Wales Stakes at Fort Erie and the Breeders' Stakes back at Woodbine. There have been just seven Triple Crown winners since the series was officially declared the Triple Crown in 1959. And there have only been five other winners of all three races in a single year since 1929.

But Queen's Plate week 2020 would not offer any of the grandeur of years past. The COVID-19 pandemic forced Woodbine to move the race to September in hopes that fans would be allowed back at the track by then. Instead, positive COVID-19 cases were creeping back up, and large gatherings remained off-limits.

Woodbine made the best of it with a virtual Queen's Plate 'at home' series of videos and virtual events. The much-anticipated post position draw, where owners and trainers get a chance to select the place in the gate they want their horse to break from, and is usually held at the track with the media and horsepeople, was also held virtually.

However, the unusual times did not dampen the spirits of Cordes and his family, as they were giddy with excitement to start their first horse in the great race.

"I remember when we were kids, watching the Queen's Plate on television with Dad," said Angela. "We would joke around about how cool it would be and what a dream it would be to have a horse in the Plate. Or even win it, like people do when they imagine winning the lottery. But you don't ever take it seriously."

In preparing feature stories for the national broadcast of the Plate on TSN, the Woodbine Entertainment television department were quick to pick up on Mighty Heart and the Cordes' story.

"About two weeks out from the Plate, we set up camera interviews with Larry and Siobhan," said Phil McSween, a television producer for Woodbine. "We even ran a picture of Mighty Heart the cat. It was amazing to meet a fellow like Larry, someone who has owned only a few horses each year for so long and now he had his first Plate starter."

There was one issue that arose for the Mighty Heart team about a week before the Plate. Justin Stein, who had ridden the colt in his maiden victory and to a recent third-place finish, chose to ride the speedy gelding Dotted Line in the Plate for trainer Sid Attard.

"It was his choice," said Carroll. "And that was fine, we just went out to look for a rider."

This was surprising news to jockey agent Pram Seebah, who was searching for a Plate mount for young Daisuke Fukumoto, who, only three weeks earlier, had won his first stakes race of his career. That win came on the filly Court Return in the Eternal Search Stakes. The winning trainer? Josie Carroll.

"I went to see trainer Sid Attard a couple of weeks before the Plate thinking that Justin Stein, who had been riding his horse Dotted Line, would be sticking with Mighty Heart," said Seebah. "When he told me Stein was riding his horse, I quickly went to talk to Josie."

Carroll had been pleased with Fukumoto's improved riding and put the young jockey on board the colt for one of his final Plate workouts.

"He loved him," said Seebah. "After the workout, he got off Mighty Heart, and he had a big smile on his face." Fukumoto was getting his first-ever Queen's Plate ride.

Mighty Heart seemed to thrive on the buzz during Plate week, at times becoming downright hard to handle during his morning regime. "The gang at the barn, they told me they had trouble even getting into his stall," said Cordes. "Normally, he is pretty docile, but Plate week, he was bucking and rearing up."

A big field of fourteen Canadian-bred three-year-olds was entered for the 161st Plate. The post position draw was a two-tiered system in which a selection order is drawn and the connections of each horse select a spot in the gate for their horse. Since the 1 1/4 mile Plate starts from the far end of the stretch run, giving horses more than one-quarter of a mile to find a position before the first turn, few were concerned about what number they drew.

Carroll drew selection order seven for Belichick and chose post three, selected eighth for Curlin's Voyage and took post ten, and with just two posts left for Mighty Heart, she took "lucky number thirteen."

In the ensuing virtual press conference, Carroll was not worried about the outside post. "I think he can get out there and put himself in position; it won't be a detriment to him. Mighty Heart is a horse that will definitely get the distance. He has improved leaps and bounds as he's learned. From his first two starts when he had no clue what he was doing, he's really become professional."

For Cordes and the other owners of Plate horses, good news came that week. They would be allowed at Woodbine to watch their horses, sequestered in the Woodbine Club dining area to enjoy lunch and the day of racing. Just before the race, the owners were ushered down to the track as the horses left the walking ring to parade on the track.

Mighty Heart, prancing with nostrils flaring, was briefly in the outdoor walking ring with the other horses but was returned to the indoor paddock for quieter surroundings.

"He walked by me, and I saw a look from him out of the corner of his eye," said Cordes. "He looked like he was saying, 'This is my day.'"

As the horses were loaded into the gate at 5:45 p.m., number thirteen Mighty Heart was made 13-to-1 by bettors watching and wagering throughout various simulcast networks that showed the race around the world.

September 12, 2020
Woodbine Racetrack
$1,000,000 Queen's Plate, 1 1/4 miles, Tapeta

Race call by Woodbine track announcer Robert Geller:

"Off and racing in the 161st running of the Queen's Plate. Great start outside by Tecumseh's War. Mighty Heart is going towards the lead and Truebelieve on the inside but going across it's Mighty Heart . . .

"Showing the way in the Queen's Plate is Mighty Heart, he leads into the backstretch by a length, Tecumseh's War and a half-length to Truebelieve, a length-and-a-half Clayton now settles beautifully in fourth . . .

"As they race three quarters in 1:12 and 3 in the Queen's Plate and Mighty Heart continues to lead the charge, a length and a quarter, Tecumseh's War. Here comes Curlin's Voyage; she's off and running, Clayton's in the centre, and they range up now.

"But it's Mighty Heart kicking right back, Mighty Heart still in front, Clayton in second, running on is Dotted Line as they corner but it's

Mighty Heart in front, the one to catch in the Queen's Plate chased by Clayton . . . but Mighty Heart is long gone!

"Mighty Heart has got the Queen's Plate completely wrapped up, and this is a dominant performance, Daisuke Fukumoto and Mighty Heart full of run by eight lengths!"

Mayhem erupted on the track's apron.

"I was grabbing my Poppy's arm, going crazy," said Jennifer. "He is always so calm and usually doesn't say a word during a race. When Willie was so far ahead, Poppy was just staring. I think because he was wondering if it was really happening."

First time past the finish line in the 161st Queen's Plate, September 12 at Woodbine, and Mighty Heart goes right to the early lead. Photo by John Watkins.

The official margin was seven-and-a-half lengths and Mighty Heart's running time of 2:01.98 was the second-fastest since the race was moved to 1 1/4 miles in 1957. The brilliant champion Izvestia won the 1990 Plate on a traditional dirt track by eleven lengths in a time of 2:01.80 (although hundredths of a second were not used to time races then).

At the finish of the Queen's Plate, Mighty Heart had won by seven and a half lengths in the second-fastest time in the history of the Plate. Jockey Fukumoto blows a kiss. Photo by John Watkins.

Behind their Covid masks, the family was screaming. Carroll and Lorimer, too.

Once Mighty Heart flew past the finish line, Cordes shouted, "YES!" as loud as he could while Angela, Jennifer, Megan, and Kim mobbed him. And while those awkward masks did their best to hide their happy faces, their squinting eyes, glittering with tears, gave away to their wide grins.

Along the railing and away from the Cordes family, Brown was sobbing and shaking with joy and disbelief.

"One of the TSN television people told me I better get my shit together as I was about to be on TV," she said, laughing.

Under orders to keep people socially distanced and certainly not hugging in mobs, helpless track security could only stand and watch.

Brown ran onto the grass course to await the return of Mighty Heart to her open arms, and Carroll was corralled by television for her reaction.

Siobhan Brown has tears of joy as Sue Lorimer congratulates her after Mighty Heart won the Plate. Photo by Will Wong.

"I was concerned for a minute or two with the quick fractions, but he looked like he was settling and doing it easily," said Carroll. "We knew he'd go all day, and he sure did. You know what, he's just a very exciting horse who's come a long way for Mr. Cordes, who's had a lot of confidence in him from the start."

Cordes had confidence in his trainer, too. "Josie had him primed and toned for this incredible performance. That is what makes her a great trainer."

What a day it was for Carroll, who not only moulded this one-eyed, quirky colt into a Plate champion but also saw Belichick pass everyone else to be second while Curlin's Voyage did well to finish fifth, picking up $20,000.

Through a remote mic, Jason Portuondo, on the TSN broadcast, was able to talk to Fukumoto moments after the victory.

"Unbelievable," said Fukumoto in his broken English. "I can't explain . . . he's feeling good today, he broke so good. I saw that nobody [was leaving] so

I just sent him and he just kept going. After the wire, he still kept going, he didn't stop there."

Cordes and his family proudly walked Mighty Heart to the infield winner's circle, with Jennifer leading the colt with her grandfather and Brown and Carroll on the other side of the horse. On the podium, Cordes was presented with the Queen's Plate trophy, made of fourteen karat yellow gold, by the Lieutenant Governor, Elizabeth Dowdeswell, representing Her Majesty the Queen. "I was just pinching myself; was this a dream?" said Cordes.

That dream was worth a cheque of $600,000.

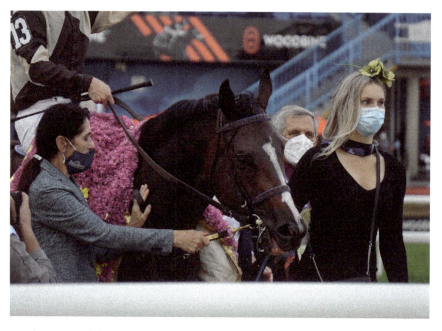

Mighty Heart is led into the Queen's Plate winner's circle by Jennifer Perrin (right) and Josie Carroll as Larry Cordes follows closely behind. Photo by Adrienne Shaw.

Cordes's son Darin, watching at his Newcastle home with friends, whooped and hollered. "I couldn't believe Dad bred a horse that was in the Plate, never mind win it."

Cheers of joy reverberated from so many places throughout the continent. Seebah, Fukumoto's young agent, watched with friends from a house not far from the track. "I was screaming at the top of my lungs; it was very, very emotional," said Seebah. "I just cried. I couldn't believe that this, winning the Plate, happened for us that quickly."

At the usually quiet Curraghmore Farm, not far from the city of Hamilton, Vera Simpson and Mike Dubé were, well, gobsmacked. "It was thrilling, incredible excitement," said Simpson. "I was so happy for Larry; he is a nice man with a wonderful family. Mighty Heart was bred by him and foaled here, and that was thrilling to get that attention." Indeed, in a matter of days, not only were Mighty Heart and Cordes featured in sports pages around the world, but Simpson and Dubé were featured in the *Hamilton Spectator*.

In Nova Scotia, Brown's mother, Gwen bubbled over with emotion for what her daughter had accomplished. "It was amazing to watch, and I am so proud of her. And to see this little one-eyed horse win the biggest Canadian race like that? It was something all of us needed in 2020."

Three days later, she watched her daughter being interviewed virtually by CBC Nova Scotia. Brown became headline news in the province's *Chronicle Herald* and *Cape Breton Post* and the talk of her little town of Groves Point.

And in Kentucky, the Mulcahys were blown away by the victory of their former student while Dana Aschinger thought of her late husband and his role in producing the breeding that resulted in Mighty Heart.

"We made sure we had the race feed on to watch the Plate," said Geoff Mulcahy. "Sandra and I were thinking it would be great if he ran well enough to get a piece of the big purse. It was incredible to see. Everyone loves the underdog story."

Aschinger watched the race from War Horse Place, the farm she shared with Gerry, the man who suggested Cordes breed Emma's Bullseye to his new stallion Dramedy. "He really believed in Dramedy; he would have been so proud."

For days following the Plate, Cordes phone wouldn't stop ringing. The beeps and blurts of text notifications were endless. "Dad's not great with his cellphone," laughed Angela. "A lot of times, we picked up his text messages and read them to him."

Cordes received congratulations and stories of winning bets from friends, relatives, and friends of relatives. Many said, "Thank you."

"He did more than just run a race and earn money," said Cordes. "People were thanking me, thanking Mighty Heart for the excitement. Friends told me they drove two hours to a betting shop to place a bet on him, the little underdog. I got calls from Ireland, Australia, England, and Germany wanting to write his story. Of course Japan, too. It went over big there because Fukumoto had never even ridden in a Queen's Plate."

Cordes never tired of telling the Mighty Heart story. "What a feeling, a once-in-a-lifetime, unbelievable thing. Anything is possible in horse racing. This CAN happen, not just for the big stables of rich owners. It can happen to anyone."

There was also a pause each time he regaled the media with the tale. "I only wish my wife and daughter and son-in-law were here to see this."

Chapter 9:

Triple Crown

RIDING THE HIGH OF Mighty Heart's Queen's Plate victory, Cordes, Carroll, and the Mighty Heart team revelled in the fun and the attention. For several mornings, there was some celebration in front of Mighty Heart's stall. Fukumoto and Seebah brought in a fancy sponge cake, and Mighty Heart was the first to eat a piece. The colt also received more stuffed animals for his stall, and there was fan mail. Jennifer even started the colt's own Instagram account.

But soon, it was time to rein things back: there was a decision to make.

The second jewel of Canada's Triple Crown, the Prince of Wales Stakes at Fort Erie, was coming up in seventeen days. That was a short time between races, especially following a horse's biggest race of his life.

At first, both Carroll and Cordes agreed that the race simply was too soon. It was on a different surface (dirt) and involved shipping ninety minutes south to the border track. The Prince of Wales is usually held at least three weeks after the Plate, but because of the Covid-delayed start of racing in Ontario, the stakes schedule had to be compressed.

Ah, but Mighty Heart had other ideas. Instead of taking several days to bounce back after that sensational Plate win, he quickly had a spring in his step. He was a star now, and he knew it.

"He just came out of the Plate so well," said Carroll, who is always very conservative with racing her horses. "Larry and I thought he deserved a chance at going for the Triple Crown."

Mighty Heart's only other start on a traditional dirt track was his first race in New Orleans when he finished fourth. However, the colt had trained well over the surface, and the challengers were not looking too tough. Other than Clayton and Tecumseh's War, both who fought on well to be third and fourth in the Plate respectively (although some ten lengths behind Mighty Heart), the other six entrants had not accomplished much. Three of them had not won a race, but with a total purse of $400,000 some owners wanted to take a shot at the champ.

Fort Erie is one of the oldest racetracks in the country, and in the last fifteen years, the most troubled. On more than one occasion, the picturesque track with its infield flora and ponds and treed perimeter was close to shutting down for good.

Built in 1896 and opened in 1897 by the Fort Erie Jockey Club under President John Hood, the track has long been a favourite of horsepeople and racing fans.

Half a century after its debut, Fort Erie was bought by E.P. Taylor, who really liked the track and thought it would make a perfect partner for his new Toronto track, Woodbine, which opened in 1956. The great Northern Dancer won his first race at Fort Erie. The Prince of Wales first ran in 1929 at Thorncliffe Park Raceway in the Leaside area of Toronto. It was moved to Fort Erie in 1959 by Taylor, who announced the official formation of the Triple Crown. Soon, the greatest Canadian Thoroughbreds were racing there, including Triple Crown champions Dance Smartly, Izvestia, With Approval, and the latest, Wando, in 2003, just to name a few.

Perhaps the most famous horse to race there, well, infamous, was Puss N Boots, who shocked everyone in September 1961 when he veered off the track and jumped into one of the infield ponds. The horse was rescued, and soon a stakes race was named after him, which is run each fall at Fort Erie. Oh, and the winning owner, trainer, and jockey have to jump in the pond to celebrate.

Like Woodbine and other tracks for other breeds of racehorses in Ontario (Standardbred and Quarter Horse), Fort Erie's business was holding its own in the 1980s and '90s. Yet, it was the introduction of slot machines into tracks that lifted horse racing to a much more prosperous level.

In seeking housing for slot machines, the provincial Liberal government approached racetracks, which, in turn, agreed for a share in the revenue to avoid potential loss out of wagering dollars to the one-armed bandits.

Casinos were built inside the tracks, and the businesses received twenty percent of the slot machine revenue that pushed up purse money for races and salaries for racetrack executives to an obscenely high amount.

The latter fact contributed to the sudden halt of the Slots At Racetracks Partner program by the Liberal government in 2012, which placed horse racing in jeopardy in the province of Ontario. That year, at the annual Queen's Plate breakfast, then-Woodbine Entertainment President Nick Eaves said there may not be any more Plates, or racing, without that small share of revenue. It was reported that Fort Erie would close for good.

Under new Ontario Premier Kathleen Wynne, a Liberal, funding for horse racing was provided, a far cry from the piles of cash it raked in during its slot heyday, but enough to keep racing afloat.

Fort Erie was not doing as well and had been through a variety of owners after the Ontario Jockey Club sold it in the early '90s with a heavy debt load.

Today, the track continues to race under the operation of the Fort Erie Live Horse Racing Consortium, made up of horsepeople and industry members with the backing of funds that all tracks received through an agreement with the province and Ontario Racing, the umbrella group of tracks in the province.

For the eighty-fifth running of the Prince of Wales, held on a Tuesday evening, once again no fans were permitted, but Cordes was allowed to bring a few more guests with him and invited Darin's son and daughter Kyle and Toni to watch the race with the family.

Brown accompanied Mighty Heart and his rival Clayton on the horse van from Woodbine to Fort Erie the morning of the race. Carroll drove to the track herself and met up with Cordes and his family in the owner's area at the track.

The butterflies were palpable.

September 29, 2020
Fort Erie Racetrack, Fort Erie
$400,000 Prince of Wales Stakes, 1 3/16 miles, dirt track

Race call from track announcer Frank Salive

They're off in the 85th running of the Prince of Wales Stakes at Fort Erie racetrack and it's a wild scrap for the early lead. First time in front of us Tecumseh's War is making a bid for the top, Truebelieve is a pace factor . . . Mighty Heart has tucked along the inside, he's now into fourth . . . the first quarter in a hotly contested 23 and 2 and Truebelieve is prompted by Dotted Line and Red Mercury, Mighty Heart is right there and just calmly waiting for developments . . . Mighty Heart and Clayton are side by side.

Clayton is ready to make a move, and there goes Clayton! Mighty Heart still in the front five, but Clayton looms bold and circles up.

The top of the stretch leader of the Prince of Wales Stakes is Clayton!

Mighty Heart now is angled off the fence and comes to call on the outside. Clayton is asked to dig deep. Here on the outside comes Mighty Heart, Mighty Heart calmly on the outside with no urging from Daisuke Fukumoto, and he goes right on by! He was never worried, Mighty Heart, mightiest again, he's two-thirds of the way to the Triple Crown!

By the finish line, seventy-six-year-old Cordes leapt in the air. "Oh my gosh, Poppy was jumping all over the place, literally jumping. That was the first time I had ever seen him do that," laughed Jennifer.

Anyone watching the TSN television feed could hear the screams of joy from Larry and his family, and Brown and Angela launched into each other with a mighty hug.

Mighty Heart had won the Princes of Wales by 2 1/2 lengths in a solid time of 1:55.59 for 1 3/16 miles as the public's beloved 4 to 5 favourite, paying out just $3.70 for every $2.00 win bet.

The jubilant team led their remarkable colt across to the winner's circle, where Carroll spoke to the media.

© 2020 forteriehorsepeople.ca

Mighty Heart streaks to the finish line in the second leg of the Canadian Triple Crown, the Prince of Wales Stakes at Fort Erie. Photo by Laurie Langley.

"Halfway around the top turn, I thought he would win the race," said Carroll. "I saw him bear down, and I know what a scrapper he is. He had bounced out of the Plate pretty good. It asks an awful lot of a horse to do that, run those two big races that close together, but I guess that is what makes the Triple Crown special if a horse can successfully do that."

Woodbine Entertainment's simulcast handicapper Jeff Bratt, watching from home in Toronto, believed it was the colt's most impressive race of the season.

"He had to race on a different surface than the Plate, but more significantly, had to wait in behind horses early while a little keen. Fukumoto was able to relax him down the backstretch, which was the key. Around the far turn, he was starting to roll and caught Clayton rather easily. For me, his effort in the Prince of Wales was even more impressive than his easy win in the Queen's Plate."

The winner's share for the Prince of Wales was $240,000, and Mighty Heart was just one more race away from Triple Crown glory.

On the quiet drive home from Fort Erie, just after 8:00 p.m., once Mighty Heart was comfortable in the van for his own ride home to Woodbine, Carroll spoke of watching Cordes after the race.

"He was just so elated. And he is such a family man; I think he was so happy to have his family all around him, his daughter and grandkids."

In her own understated manner, Carroll discussed her own feelings of the day and the race. "It was pretty neat. But I could see this horse getting better all the time, and the more he learns about running, the better he gets. Before the race, I told Daisuke that I didn't expect them to be alone on the lead today. I thought there would be more speed. Early on in the race, I was okay with where he was, but by the end of the backstretch you're thinking, 'Okay, we gotta find a way through here.' Daisuke did the right thing, he tipped him out and found a path, and I thought, for a young rider, he rode him very professionally."

With October just around the corner, Carroll had twenty-five days to get Mighty Heart ready for the most demanding leg of the Triple Crown, the 1 1/2 mile Breeders' Stakes on the grass at Woodbine.

By the end of the first week of October, while people were spending more time inside rather than outside, COVID-19 cases were on the rise again. Ontario Premier Doug Ford announced the second wave had started and implemented a mask-wearing mandate, restricting the number of people in bars and restaurants. Not much could be done, however. When Breeders' Stakes weekend came, Ontario saw new records in Covid cases upwards of one thousand a day.

Angela called the ride they were on with Mighty Heart 'surreal,' and she enjoyed watching her dad revel in the attention. The pandemic was still very worrisome, especially for seniors, but the Cordes family felt blessed.

"This was obviously a first-time experience for our family," said Angela. "We have never been in that situation before, and we were all living it together. What an honour it was to be able to say, here we are, a regular family, nobodies in horse racing really, and all of a sudden our horse has won the Plate and the Prince of Wales. We had so many people congratulating us. Even our priest from church called us—he wanted to buy tickets to the Breeders' and watch it with us. But it turned out no one was able to go that day."

A young fan, Hadley, sent Mighty Heart a letter and a stuffed animal. "I ride a horse named Goose. He isn't as fast as you. I love watching you race." Photo courtesy of the Cordes' family.

Interest in Mighty Heart's quest for the Triple Crown exploded, especially since the colt would seemingly take to the grass as his sire Dramedy did. He had tried turf once, in one of those bizarre races in New Orleans, but he was a better horse heading into the Breeders'.

The first frost of the fall glistened on Woodbine's E.P. Taylor turf course on the morning of October 17 when Mighty Heart was to have a workout on the grass to get accustomed to the surface. It was barely a single degree

Celsius on a cloudless day when Cordes walked into the main entrance of Woodbine. He had driven for more than ninety minutes to get there to see his colt prep on the turf. He had to do a little finagling to get in as a security guard, under orders not to let anyone into the track unless they worked there, asked many questions while he took Cordes's temperature. But the guard knew of Mighty Heart and told Cordes to go ahead.

Mighty Heart and Fukumoto came down the outside of the turf course with stablemate Curlin's Voyage, who was pointing to a filly race on the grass. You could see their breath as they galloped past Cordes, Carroll, and a Woodbine television crew. It was a strong workout.

A few days before Mighty Heart's date with destiny, Woodbine Entertainment held an invitation-only media scrum at Carroll's barn with social distancing and Covid protocols in place. All of the province's top television, radio, and newsprint media were on hand to film and photograph the colt, who was picking at some grass on the front lawn. For many of the reporters, just the sight of a horse missing an eye was a first, never mind a horse on the cusp of history.

In the days before the final leg of the Triple Crown, the Mighty Heart team met with dozens of media outlets. Photo by Michael Burns.

Sadly, the rise in Covid cases and the ensuing restrictions meant that owners were no longer permitted at the track once again. It was tremendously disappointing for Larry and his family to not watch their colt race for the Triple Crown at Woodbine. Instead, son Darin hosted a twenty-five-person gathering in the backyard at his Newcastle home. Woodbine sent batches of flowers and a healthy supply of Mumm's champagne as well as a small television crew to film the festivities.

Ten other horses were entered to race against Mighty Heart in the Breeders', including Clayton and a host of longshots. But one colt, who was on the other side of Carroll's barn from Mighty Heart, was the one that Cordes greatly respected.

"Josie's other horse Belichick, he was second in the Plate; he is the one who concerns me the most in the Breeders'," said Cordes.

October 24, 2020
Woodbine Racetrack
$401,200 Breeders' Stakes, 1 1/2 miles turf

Race call from Woodbine track announcer Robert Geller

"Locked up, and they're off! Mighty Heart is one of the best away . . . he's trying to get across and he does, he's gone to the front! The pace is solid as the top three have torn away, and Mighty Heart is galloping at a very fast pace here from Kunal.

"Mighty Heart is being engaged by Kunal as they go up the back-stretch in the Breeders' Stakes.

Trying to relax is Mighty Heart, he's gone back in front as they race along to the five-eighths as Mighty Heart goes away by a length and a half . . . Belichick is starting to wind up on the outside . . . now Mighty Heart is joined by others, Told It All ranges up on the outside, three eighths left in the Breeders' Stakes and Told It All and Belichick race up to Mighty Heart . . . Mighty Heart on the inside trying to fight back . . ."

Mighty Heart was pumped up at the start of the Breeders' Stakes, racing straight to the early lead. Photo by John Watkins.

"It's okay Willie, good boy, good boy." Those were the words that the few people trackside at the finish of the Breeders' could hear. Brown still cheered on the hero as he crossed the finish line a tired seventh, well behind his stablemate, Belichick, who took advantage of the hot, early pace and a grass course dampened by some of the week's rain. Longshot Meyer, whose stablemate Kunal had pushed Mighty Heart to go so fast early, finished second.

Even being a major stake, there was a hush from the small group of media, track staff, and horsepeople.

Far away in Newcastle, Cordes and his family fell silent, crushed that Mighty Heart had gone so fast and too soon in the race, being pushed along by 101 to 1 longshot Kunal.

"Ah, its a horse race," said Larry. "It was just a disappointment, not just for me but for the fans hoping for a Triple Crown winner.

"But you can't run that speed for the first half and still expect to be there at the end of a mile and a half; he would have to be a super horse."

Carroll, interviewed after the race by national television, almost looked uncomfortable talking about Belichick's big win, coming in just his fourth start.

"It's very bittersweet. It is exciting to win with this horse, but how often do you have a horse with a chance to win the Triple Crown?"

"I told Daisuke, let's see how the race folds out, and if you make the lead, watch your fractions, you're going to need to know what kind of time you're going in as it's a long, long race. He broke well and got the lead, but unfortunately, another horse dogged him, and he couldn't get the horse to come off the bridle and relax. Mighty Heart ran his little heart out."

Fukumoto, approached by television after the race, had difficulty keeping up a brave face. He had been confident in his colt, but the young rider had let his strong-willed mount get caught up in a disastrous speed battle.

His agent Seebah felt bad for his rider.

"I know he was disappointed in himself. You know, there had been a bit of chatting in the days before the race that the speed horse Kunal was in the race to go fast for his stablemate, Meyer. You try not to let other people's horses distract you from your own game, but things like that happen in every race. Look, we had the whole Triple Crown journey, right to the end. And to win all three races on three different surfaces, so many things have to go right. But to win two of the races, it was amazing."

Brown, much like Cordes, took it hard, feeling as if she had let the fans down.

"I was upset," said Brown. "I put it all on myself, but then again, I have my routine every day with my horses. You take care of them and make sure they are not stressed when they go over to race. But then to watch him go so fast, so early, you feel helpless. But he never gave up. He always gives everything he has."

Later on Breeders' night, Cordes called Brown and told her what a great job she had done with his colt. They shared thoughts and a few tears. It had been a hell of a ride.

Chapter 10:

Horse of the Year

MIGHTY HEART RACED ONCE more in 2020 following his incredible run through the Canadian Triple Crown. The Ontario Derby on November 21 was an 'open' race and a Grade Three, which meant that American horses were eligible, and Cordes and Carroll wanted to see how the colt would do in tougher competition. The 1 1/8 mile race on the Woodbine Tapeta attracted a strong challenger in Field Pass, a rugged grey colt who had won stakes races in Florida and Kentucky. Belichick was there too.

With Cordes still smarting about Fukumoto's error in tactics in the Breeders' Stakes, Woodbine's leading jockey Rafael Hernandez was hired to partner the popular colt.

Made the favourite by the 'virtual' fans—the province was heading towards another full lockdown—Mighty Heart jumped out to an early lead and was still in front, turning into the stretch. But he looked tired, and coming to the finish, he slipped back to fourth place, a few lengths behind Field Pass. Belichick finished second.

"His blood work was all good, and he was acting good before the race," said Carroll. "But I think his campaign had knocked him out more than he showed. The Triple Crown series, it takes its toll."

It was time for the colt to get a good rest.

Meanwhile the pandemic raged on. The situation was eerily similar to when racing was shut down right after Mighty Heart's second race in New Orleans in the spring. Just one day after Mighty Heart's Ontario derby run, the final three weeks of the Woodbine season were cancelled by the province's latest lockdown of all outdoor activities.

Positive COVID-19 cases in Ontario were close to two thousand daily, and by January, it would be at a staggering four thousand. Intensive care units were full, and the death rate was tragically close to five thousand. The vaccine rollout was beginning, and long-term care patients were the first to receive them, but Christmas and New Year's gatherings were cancelled, and schools would soon be shuttered again.

The border to the U.S. remained closed to non-essential travel. With that country's COVID-19 death and case rates seemingly out of control, most Ontario horsepeople, who usually spend the winter in Florida, elected to stay home.

Carroll didn't have that option; she had horses still in racing mode and had events pegged for them in Florida through the winter.

"I had young horses that needed to race down there," said Carroll. "I couldn't take all my staff with me because I didn't want any of them to get stuck down there and not get back into Canada in the spring. I took my assistant Sue, and one of my exercise riders, Melanie Pinto. I had to hire all new staff when I got down to Palm Meadows Training Centre."

To make matters worse, although Carroll got across the border, her partner Charlie, who would be helping out with the stable, was deemed 'non-essential' by a strict border security person and was turned back.

For the first time in their twenty-seven years together, Carroll and Charlie would be apart for an extended period.

Mighty Heart was vanned to Ocala in central Florida, a popular vacation spot for racehorses and Michael Cooke's Cookes Town Farm. Cooke, who had once worked at the famed Windfields Farm in Oshawa, was very familiar with his new star resident and turned him out into the lush grass paddocks at his farm for a couple of months of fun in the sun.

Brown packed up for her drive back home to Cape Breton, but she first had to apply for re-entry through New Brunswick and into Nova Scotia due to closed provincial borders. She would spend a restful and "a little boring" winter at home.

Des McMahon returned to his family in Fort Erie while jockey Fukumoto went back home to Japan for two months to be with his family. Before travelling, Fukumoto received an invitation to ride races in Bahrain in the Persian Gulf. His agent, Pram Seebah, stayed home in Brampton to ride out the lockdown.

Cordes and his family also settled in for a long winter's stay at home, but there was still the business to run. There were also a few of his younger horses to visit at Ballycroy Training Centre, and his one remaining broodmare, Trigger Finger, would need a mate for the spring, so Cordes got to work researching stallions.

But it wasn't long before early preparation for the 2021 Woodbine season was underway again at farms around the province. And by March 1st, the Woodbine backstretch was once again becoming full of horses. Mighty Heart had returned to Carroll's watchful eye at Palm Meadows and began early training. He was a four-year-old now, a bit stronger, and a lot more cocky.

On April 15, the annual Sovereign Awards, presented by the Jockey Club of Canada, were held virtually for the second consecutive year. Since the 1970s, the Sovereigns honour the previous year's top horses and horsepeople through voting by industry members across the country.

Cordes, who was fairly confident Mighty Heart would be named the Champion Three-Year-Old Colt of the year, watched the 'ceremony' with his family in Uxbridge on a big-screen television. Mighty Heart was indeed voted the top sophomore colt of the year, but it was the big award of the night, the Horse of the Year, that Cordes dearly wanted for his colt. There was stiff competition for that honour from the brilliant older sprinter Pink Lloyd, a previous Horse of the Year who had completed another fantastic racing season with four stakes victories.

Glenn Sikura, Jockey Club of Canada president, appeared on-screen close to 9:30 that evening with the envelope in his hand. When he opened it and got ready to name the Horse of the Year, a video of Mighty Heart's Plate victory was shown, and the Cordes family went wild.

The vote was virtually unanimous; the colt had won the biggest Canadian horse racing trophy of them all.

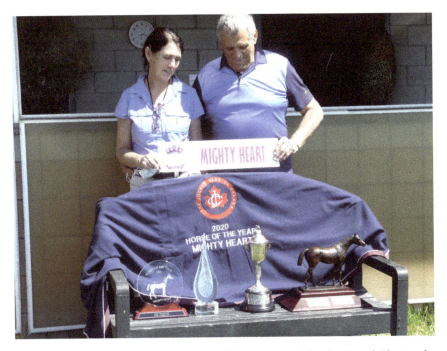

Josie Carroll and Larry show off Mighty Heart's hardware, including his Queen's Plate trophy (second from right) and Horse of the Year trophy (far right). Photo by Jennifer Morrison.

The texts, calls, and notes on social media poured in again, not just to Cordes but to Carroll, who was watching from Florida. One letter to Carroll and the racing community, sent to the racing website Canadian Thoroughbred came from Colorado, and Ruth Schmidt, a former employee of Carroll's at Woodbine.

"Mighty Heart's story was a bright light in a year that has been filled with darkness, uncertainty, and fear for all. He brought excitement, joy, and collective hope. Watching and cheering for the one-eyed wonder gave many of us a short but most welcome reprieve from the challenges of navigating our daily lives in unprecedented times. His success is due to countless hours of hard work and dedication by a whole group of people. And at the helm, the unwavering hand of Josie. Under her watchful eyes, with her knowledge, skill and experience, her trainees grow and thrive until she deems them ready to step into the starting gate."

Carroll was much more humble.

"Everybody deserves credit for this horse doing the amazing things that he did," she said. "There was a lot of work that went into getting this guy there, not just one person, the entire team."

Carroll's own remarkable season of training horses in 2020 saw her nominated for a Sovereign Award for Outstanding Trainer, but she surprisingly just missed that honour to the track's leading race-winning trainer Mark Casse.

The Sovereign Awards virtual ceremony was expected to usher in the 2021 racing season, scheduled for April 17th, but little had changed with the provincial COVID-19 restrictions. In fact, during the same week of the Sovereign Awards, Ontario had set a disheartening record: the most positive cases in a single day of 4,456. Vaccine roll-out was slow. Variants of the Covid virus had found a way into the province. Premier Ford had already declared another state of emergency and another stay-at-home order was in place until June.

Horses and their people had already started shipping into Woodbine in early March, and training was in full swing. But no firm start date was on the horizon, and when April 17th came and went, horsepeople became uneasy. "It was incredibly difficult to train horses when we didn't know, once again, when racing would start," said Carroll.

Carroll had returned home by mid-April but had left horses at Keeneland racecourse in Kentucky with her assistant Sue Lorimer. Mighty Heart was ready to race. On the day Woodbine had been scheduled to open, Mighty Heart made his four-year-old debut in a tough allowance race (races one level below stakes events) at Keeneland on the dirt. Meeting older horses for the first time, Mighty Heart finished a gallant third.

Then, a week later, Woodbine's barn area had its own COVID-19 outbreak after more than a year of being virus-free. The outbreak was contained to two barns, including that of Sovereign Award-nominated trainer Kevin Attard, who himself became ill. Horses in the affected barns had to be moved to other trainers or nearby farms as horsepeople were sent home to quarantine for two weeks.

Jim Lawson pushed for a mobile vaccine clinic for horsepeople. In early May he would eventually get it, soon after the Kentucky Derby was run at

Churchill Downs with fans in attendance. Through four days of the clinic, which served the residents of the Rexdale area and track workers, the majority of horsepeople had received their first vaccine.

Lawson's battle was not over. Speaking to horsepeople through an online forum in late May, the frustration in Lawson's voice was evident. Golf courses were re-opening, and yet, the Ontario Ministry of Health had kept horse racing on the banned list (but allowed for training), which did not make sense to Lawson or to horsepeople, since the same staff who were training the horses at Woodbine would be the ones walking them over to race.

Some trainers started to ship their horses out to tracks in the U.S., and Woodbine's perennial leading trainer Mark Casse, who had some at Woodbine, was unwilling to send his full stable until there was a firm plan to allow racing.

The fact that the National Hockey League was well underway with games for Canadian teams, including the Toronto Maple Leafs at the Scotiabank Centre, was also a bone of contention for Lawson.

"Horse racing is an outdoor activity, and we have been trying to get the provincial Ministry of Health to have a comprehensive understanding of what we do and how we do it. I continue to be concerned and frustrated. We have had very good conversations with the Toronto Board of Health, and the Premier's office has been supportive. There simply has been no dialogue with the provincial Ministry of Health. And I am tired of giving our horsepeople hope."

It wasn't until after the stay-at-home order expired on June 2nd that Lawson began to believe racing was getting closer to starting up. Tracks in western Canada in B.C., Alberta, and Manitoba were already underway with their race meetings.

Meanwhile, Mighty Heart travelled to famed Churchill Downs following his Keeneland race and was pegged to compete in another allowance event before returning to Canada.

But when Carroll saw the early nominations for an upcoming $150,000 (U.S.) stakes race, she was intrigued. "I looked at the horses he would be meeting, and I thought maybe he could be a contender." Cordes agreed, but since Mighty Heart had not originally been nominated to the May 29th race, called the Blame Stakes (named after a Breeders' Cup Classic winner), and he had to be supplemented to the race at the cost of $2,500 (U.S.).

Racing over the Churchill Downs dirt for the first time, Mighty Heart and his American-based jockey James Graham pressed the early front runners to the turn for home. Just when it looked like he was beginning to tire, his mighty heart kicked in. With favourite Night Ops on his outside and second favourite Sprawl to his inside, Mighty Heart refused to give in. He battled on and won by a nose.

Anyone who called the Cordes family home immediately following the race got an earful of hoots and hollers, yet another joyous moment with their remarkable colt.

"He just reached out for more like he usually does," said Carroll, who was watching from home with Charlie and their new puppy, Jackson. "That was really, very exciting; he is so gutsy."

Mighty Heart (middle) bravely fends off Night Ops and Sprawl (inside) to win the Blame Stakes in front of the famous twin spires at Churchill Downs, May 29th.
Photo by Jamie Newell.

A few hours following that hard-fought victory, Mighty Heart and assistant Sue Lorimer returned to Woodbine. Brown, who had made her way back to Ontario from Nova Scotia a few weeks earlier, was there with Carroll to greet the colt as he stepped off the van.

A freshly bedded stall, a pile of carrot tops—his favourite treat—and plenty of hay was ready for him in his stall.

Cordes had not seen his prized colt for more than seven months, but on a warm and sunny June 10th morning, two days before racing in Ontario was able to start up, Cordes drove into the Woodbine barn area with special permission from the track. The strict COVID-19 protocols still did not allow for owners or visitors to the backstretch, but he had been asked to do a photoshoot with his colt.

As Cordes stepped into the shedrow, armed with donuts for the barn staff, and of course, carrot tops for his champion, he spotted the colt's crooked white-blaze peeking out of his stall. Mighty Heart turned to look at him.

Cordes quietly walked into Mighty Heart's stall and greeted him with some scratches behind his ears and down his blazed face. As if remembering this was the person who brought him into the world, Mighty Heart rested his head in Cordes's arms. They shared a quiet moment. And carrots.

The champ was home.

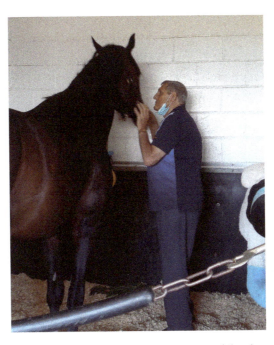

June 2021, Larry Cordes spends a quiet moment with his champion.
Photo by Jennifer Morrison.

Chapter 11:
Canada Day 2021

A SENSE OF NORMALCY arrived in Ontario on June 11th, at the stroke of midnight when Step 1 of the 'Roadmap to Reopening' began. On June 12th, Woodbine opened its racing season, and excited but anxious horsepeople were able to take their horses to the races. With about seventy percent of the province's citizens having received their first COVID-19 vaccine, whether it was Pfizer, Moderna or AstraZeneca, Premier Doug Ford and health officials were confident that a slow reopening of the economy could begin. It had been a long, sad, and scary fourteen months for the world. While Ontario was much slower than all of North America in its easing of restrictions, much of the fear and frustration for the thousands involved in horse racing was left behind when the Ontario-bred filly Five Days in May galloped to victory in the first race of the Woodbine season. There still weren't any spectators or owners permitted, but racing was back in business.

"For those of us who worked in the industry in Ontario, it felt excruciating to be in another lockdown this year, due to a third wave, that placed our own Woodbine season in jeopardy," said track announcer Robert Geller. "As trying as 2020 had been, it was almost inconceivable that 2021 could be worse, yet that is how it started off for us, racing delayed even longer than the previous year."

In the Cordes camp, the family was staying safe and still riding the high of Mighty Heart's brilliant win at Churchill Downs, but there was more excitement in the works. Cordes took out a lease on a twenty-five-acre farm in Uxbridge, close to their home so that the family could stable their racehorses, riding horses, and various other equine friends collected by Jennifer and Megan. The farm was christened Horizon Acres (after Cordes' first business), where Megan and Jennifer were soon caring for almost a dozen residents, training younger riding horses and going for rides on their own horses.

Cordes and Carroll made plans for Mighty Heart's next race, the prestigious Dominion Day Stakes, a Grade Three race, on July 1st.

Inaugurated in 1953, the Dominion Day—named for the Confederation of Canada on July 1, 1867—has been won by some of the greatest horses in Canadian history. To name a few, Ace Marine, the 1955 Horse of the Year; Kennedy Road the 1973 Horse of the Year and the great mare Glorious Song, a champion not only in Canada but the U.S. who won in it in 1980 and '81.

Two Kentucky Derby winners even came up to Woodbine and won the Dominion Day: Decidedly in 1963 and Funny Cide in 2006.

It would be a fitting return race at Woodbine for the Canadian hero.

Cordes was also getting excited about his three younger horses who stabled with Carroll. He didn't have to wait long to see one of them race as Trigger's Bay, the three-year-old who had shown promise in his one race in 2020, was entered on the second day of the Woodbine season, June 13th.

Racing against eleven other promising horses seeking their first career win, Trigger's Bay and his jockey Luis Contreras moved up wide on the turn of the seven-furlong race, took the lead in the stretch, and were just caught in the final strides by HC Holiday. It was a super comeback race for the gelding. He would win his next race on July 2nd, daring Cordes and his family to have thoughts about having an entrant in the 2021 Queen's Plate, scheduled for August 22nd.

Unfortunately, Trigger's Bay suffered a leg injury and Cordes's two other potential runners for 2021 who had only been in training at Woodbine for a short time were sent to their farm. Mighty Heart's three-year-old half-sister, Evelyn's Delight, had been plagued by several minor physical issues and went to Horizon Acres. The two-year-old colt Trizmo, a half brother to Trigger's Bay, was getting too hard to handle and was sent to Ballycroy to be gelded and to mature. Cordes once again was left with just one horse in his stable for 2021, his prized Mighty Heart.

As Canada Day neared, so too did Step 2 of the province's re-opening plan. The prevalence of the COVID-19 virus was certainly dissipating, but there were still dangerous variants to respect, particularly the much more contagious Delta variant. But case numbers across the country were steadily dropping thanks to the concentrated efforts of health workers to get vaccines into the arms of millions.

Ontario moved to Stage 2 a few days earlier than projected, June 30th, and by then, there were just over two hundred cases per day in the province and just over four hundred in the country daily.

With the news of the early move to the next phase of reopening—meaning hair salons could finally reopen and larger gatherings outdoors were permitted—Woodbine announced that a restricted number of fans would be able to register to attend the Canada Day races. The outdoor restaurant, Champions, overlooking the track, would be open, and of course, owners were welcomed back.

Hours before the gates to the track were even open fans had lined up, registration in hand, and ready to grab a seat in the Woodbine grandstand.

Mighty Heart had prepared for the Dominion Day Stakes with a couple of workouts, in addition to daily galloping, and it was evident the colt was not only maturing but getting stronger. Cordes and Carroll also brought Daisuke Fukumoto back to the team; he would ride the colt in the race.

Mighty Heart's competition for the 1 1/8th mile race on the Tapeta surface included two tough fellows from the Mark Casse barn: the well-travelled March to the Arch, who had won important races on the grass throughout the last three seasons; and Skywire, who won two of Woodbine's graded races for older horses in 2020.

The morning of Dominion Day, Mighty Heart knew it was race day. As with most horses who will race in the afternoon, they are hand-walked. He spent the training hours sleeping in his stall, snoring, but when Brown began to get him ready for his race, 'Willie' gave her all that she could handle. She would soon have half a dozen marks on her arms from his playful nips.

As Brown led Mighty Heart over to the Woodbine saddling enclosure, she could hear the hum of fans in the grandstand. Even Mighty Heart was doing a lot of looking around at the sight of spectators along the railing leading out to the track. He had not seen a crowd of people at his races since he was in New Orleans at the beginning of his career.

"There he is," said one woman, who pointed out the colt to her family as he walked by. "Good luck Mighty Heart!"

Among the spectators were sisters Julie Wright and Denise Bond, just two of many in attendance wearing Mighty Heart t-shirts made up by Old Smoke Clothing, a company based in Saratoga, New York, during the colt's Triple Crown run. On the shirt, it said, "Anything Is Possible with a Mighty Heart."

Old Smoke Clothing in Saratoga Springs, New York made up Mighty Heart t-shirts during his Triple Crown quest. Photo from OldSmokeClothing.com.

The sisters have been in love with horse racing since they can remember. Each has some small involvement; Bond owns small shares in a couple of Standardbred horses, while Wright's photography prowess has seen her photos in many racing publications.

But neither had seen a horse race in person in almost two years, and they had never seen Mighty Heart up close.

"In any year, he would have been a great role model for overcoming adversity," said Wright. "But in 2020, he was that and more—a way for racing fans to participate in something resembling normality by being able to cheer him on. Finally getting to see him in the flesh was a great thrill and especially poignant as it was the first day fans were allowed back at Woodbine. There's just no substitute for seeing a champion up close and personal."

Cordes was able to bring a few more of his family and friends to Woodbine with restrictions eased. There were nearly two dozen in the Mighty Heart group, many of them seeing their friend's horse for the first time.

For the first time since 2019, fans were allowed at Woodbine on Canada Day 2021, and got to see Mighty Heart compete in the Dominion Day Stakes. Photo by Jennifer Morrison.

July 2, 2021

Woodbine Racetrack
$171,300 Dominion Day Stakes (Grade 3), 1 1/8 miles, Tapeta

Race call from track announcer Robert Geller

"And they're off and Mighty Heart goes straight to the lead . . . Mighty Heart has gone across to the rail to lead now by a length and slowing them right down is jockey Daisuke Fukumoto. March to the Arch is not having it, he's coming up three wide . . . It's a tactical race as March to the Arch is now pushing the pace, Mighty Heart is in front . . . Mighty Heart is on top and March to the Arch is breathing down his neck and they pick up the tempo . . . Mighty Heart's in front as they turn for home, he's not giving up. Mighty Heart is coming on to win, the Queen's Plate winner is back at Woodbine with a win!"

In front of an adoring crowd at Woodbine on July 1, 2021, Mighty Heart powered to victory in the $171,300 Dominion Day Stakes, a Grade 3 event. Photo by Santino DiPaola.

With a couple of underhanded taps of Fukumoto's whip, Mighty Heart fended off stern challenges by March to the Arch and Malibu Mambo in the stretch run of the Dominion Day. He swished his tail and powered away to win while Cordes and his entourage screamed for joy, easily drowning out fans in the stands.

In fact, they were so loud Geller admits to being distracted from his race call. "The team of Mighty Heart, spurred on by his committed groom, Siobhan Brown, began to rouse as if it was Queen's Plate day all over again though this time I could not help but hear them. I had to concentrate more than ever to make sure I rounded the call out well. I had almost forgotten what it was like to hear a roar from a crowd as a field turned for home."

The win was fantastic, Cordes would say after the race, but the presence of spectators finally at the track, particularly his family and friends, made it even more special. "This made it so much better. And there were lots of his followers in the crowd too. This is the epitome."

Surrounded by family and friends, Larry Cordes (white shirt) celebrated Mighty Heart's Canada Day victory. Photo by Jennifer Morrison.

Carroll was very pleased. She has been the curator of many champion racehorses, but a one-eyed horse owned by a man who has been through so much love and loss in his life? Extra special.

"It has been very exciting," said Carroll. "Larry is such a family man, and he is so happy to share this with everyone."

It is indeed a labour of love for Carroll and her team. The highs can be very high and the lows, devastating. Her skills, patience, and instincts with racehorses have put her firmly in place as one of the most respected horsepeople in the sport.

"The passion for what I do is always there. But you need good, dedicated people working with you who are detail-oriented. You need good horses and good owners who trust that you will do the best you can when they put their horse in your hands. With Mighty Heart, it has been amazing how far he has come. So many people have been a part of his development."

Carroll hopes there are many exciting times to come with the champ. "The best part about Mighty Heart is drawing attention to our sport and how great it is. You hope that his success and following brings more people into the business."

Cordes would be inundated with cards, letters and stuffed animals throughout 2021. One young woman, Alexandra, from the Canadian Forces Base in Trenton, sent a long letter and some CFB keepsakes. Cordes sent her one of Mighty Heart's shoes.

When Siobhan Brown gets a few moments to herself after a long day at the barn, she too shakes her head in amazement and pride. The similarities between her journey through a disability and that of Mighty Heart are not lost on her.

"I hope by sharing my story of living with a disability, if I could inspire one person to try something they thought they couldn't do, it would be a success. Mighty Heart has played a tremendous role in helping me become a better groom. I've only been at this [for] a few years and there is still so much for me to learn, but working with him has helped build my confidence. I have a bad habit of doubting myself, but when I see what I have helped him accomplish, it brings a sense of pride."

The Loose Girth Grooming and Treat Store in Guelph, Ontario, made up special horse treats for Mighty Heart following his Dominion Day Stakes win. Photo by Hayley Badner.

More than a year after Mighty Heart made his first career start on the cusp of a deadly world pandemic, the Cordes family still feel like it has been a wonderful dream.

"We are a family that is so close, and to see Poppy and how proud he is, how excited he is, it has been an incredible experience." said Megan.

Cordes has always been in awe of the beauty and desire of the Thoroughbred and has enjoyed every minute of his life with horses that began all those years ago with that black and white pony.

"I have been in love with the Thoroughbred because they are athletes in the very best sense. Their physical make-up and their alertness are what attracts me."

Now Cordes and his little one-eyed colt are in the pages of the history books in one of the oldest sports in Canada.

"To see this little foal grow up, show his athletic ability, and become what he has, I just thank him. Through this pandemic, there was not a lot to look forward to, and I think Mighty Heart gave so many a lift of happiness, desire, and anticipation. He certainly has given my family a lot of joy."

A mighty heart, indeed. ♥

Photo by Brittany Troxtell.

Epilogue

A LIGHT BUT COLD and steady rain fell over Woodbine on November 14 when Siobhan Brown led Mighty Heart from the barn to the track for the afternoon's eighth race, the Autumn Stakes worth $197,750. The Autumn, an important race for older horses, was also one of the oldest races on the Woodbine calendar. It was first run in 1902 at Old Woodbine and won by a horse named Janice. In the 1920's, the Autumn Stakes lured the great American horse Exterminator, affectionately known as "Old Bones", who won three consecutive editions in 1920, '21 and '22.

As Brown and hotwalker Gerald arrived at the saddling enclosure, Brown was nervous. Mighty Heart, who was now going by the more mature nickname of 'William', was on an unlucky losing streak.

Following his Dominion Day Stakes victory on Canada Day, Mighty Heart continued with a schedule which saw him race once a month. In August, the colt was vanned to Mountaineer Park in West Virginia for the $200,000 (US) West Virginia Governor's Stakes, a Grade Three event at one and one sixteenth miles on a traditional dirt surface. He was meeting up with Sprawl again, whom he had defeated in the Blame Stakes at Churchill Downs in May. This time, however, Sprawl darted out to the lead, kept Mighty Heart and Daisuke Fukumoto to his outside and fended off the Canadian champ all the way to the finish, beating him by just over one length.

Back at Woodbine for the Grade Three Seagram Cup Stakes on September 11, Mighty Heart was heavily favoured to defeat four rivals including two from the barn of leading trainer Mark Casse. But Fukumoto elected to take a firm hold of Mighty Heart early in the race, allowing Tap It to Win to coast on a slow, early lead. Mighty Heart could not catch him.

Cordes was frustrated. He knew his colt had simply not been given the best chance to show his talent. Fukumoto would be replaced by one of Woodbine's all-time leading jockeys, Patrick Husbands, for the $155,100 Durham Cup Stakes on October 10. His competition included the classy Sir Winston, winner of the 2019 Belmont Stakes, the third jewel of the American Triple Crown.

But the bad luck continued. As Mighty Heart made his move between rivals on the final turn for home one of his shoes somehow ripped off his foot, causing the colt to lose momentum. Husbands would say later, "I couldn't get him going again." Mighty Heart fought on bravely to finish fourth behind a Special Forces, Sir Winston and Halo Again.

Cordes and Carroll decided to do a thorough physical on the colt to ensure he had not injured himself from racing on three shoes.

"We x-rayed him from the tip of his ears to the bottom of his feet," said Cordes. "The veterinarian took 55 pictures and she told us he was perfect. She said you would never know he had ever raced."

The Autumn was the final race for Mighty Heart of the 2021 Woodbine season, which would wrap up December 5. Business had been good at the track as COVID-19 restrictions on the number of spectators had all been lifted and more than 75 percent of Ontarians had been fully vaccinated. The daily case count of positive tests for the virus still hovered in the 450-500 range but the majority of those were in people who were not fully, or only partially vaccinated.

Cordes brought a group of twenty-five to Woodbine for the Autumn Stakes to watch Mighty Heart and Patrick Husbands take on six, tough horses in the Grade Two race including Special Forces and Sir Winston. This time, Husbands and Carroll decided on the same pre-race strategy; let Mighty Heart roll.

And roll he did. From his outside post, Mighty Heart galloped to the front of the field and was going fairly quickly. He had a one-length lead over Halo Again coming into the stretch run while Sir Winston was gearing up for a late charge. But Mighty Heart, head cocked slightly to the left, would not relinquish his lead.

November 14, 2021
Woodbine Racetrack
$197,750 Autumn Stakes (Grade 2), 1 1/16 miles, Tapeta

Race call excerpt from track announcer Robert Geller

And they're off. A great start and away well, Mighty Heart. And Mighty Heart is showing a lot of dash in the early stages to go for the lead. It's Mighty Heart, so far the first mission achieved, from the outside post to the rail to lead the field. Mighty Heart has his running shoes on today, he's in front.

I think Mighty Heart is doing everything right so far, he's two lengths in front. Now the challenge from Halo Again, Mighty Heart a length, holding on. Sir Winston down the outside, Mighty Heart! Mighty Heart has done it!

The cheering and chanting filled the Woodbine grandstand as Mighty Heart came into the winner's circle. The rain continued to pelt down on Cordes and his two dozen friends as well as brave fans who ran outside to grab some photos of the colt. Husbands was beaming. "Today I put him in the race [early] and he showed he was a true champion." Big words from a man who has won eight Sovereign Awards as Canada's Outstanding Jockey and has ridden dozens of the best horses in the land through the last two decades.

Carroll and Cordes felt vindicated; Mighty Heart's time of 1:42.51 missed the track record by 0.35 of a second. "A once in a lifetime horse," said Cordes, whose excited guests were made up of many first-time visitors to a racetrack. "Ordinary people like me and his followers are getting the kick of their life watching him race."

Back at the barn after having undergone post-race urine collection at the Woodbine test barn—required for all winning horses—Mighty Heart voraciously attacked his hay, pausing only when a visitor approached with his favourite mints. Brown, emotionally and physically weary, gave her colt a big hug and then got to work applying his four new fluffy leg bandages. Carroll, who sent out two other winners on the busy afternoon, did a check on the colt and all of her other horses. "He's an exciting horse and they don't come along very often," said Carroll. "He had his handicap to overcome but nothing fazes him."

Mighty Heart, Carroll and Brown would soon be on their way to Palm Meadows training centre in Florida for the winter with perhaps a race or two pencilled in for their star colt at Gulfstream Park. Cordes made a plan to race Mighty Heart one more season at Woodbine, as a five-year-old in 2022, and then will retire him for stallion duty. He is already in talks with stud farms in Ontario and can't wait for his champion to pass on that mighty heart.

On a rainy and cold November 14, 2021, MIghty Heart heads to the crowded Woodbine winner's circle after winning the prestigious Autumn Stakes. Many followers of the champion (such as the person in the red coat, top left) braved the elements to watch him in action - Mr. Will Wong photo

Acknowledgements

MY LIFELONG DREAM HAS been fulfilled.

I began writing horse stories in grade school and some were long enough to be mini-books. I have been lucky enough to write news articles and feature stories on horse racing, plus be a published public handicapper, as a career. My love for racing began very much as it did for Josie Carroll—I was obsessed with racing stories and track entries in the newspapers. I made selections for races, recorded them in binders and checked the results the next day.

I have always wanted to write a book. There are dozens of notebooks and computer files in my home office with the beginnings of book ideas. Like a really slow racehorse, those ideas barely made it out of the gate.

But out of nowhere came the horse and his people who would change my writing career. Mighty Heart's victory in the Queen's Plate on September 12th, 2020 was stunning and inspiring. A one-eyed colt winning a famous horse race in the midst of a world pandemic that made so many of us scared and depressed. His story, and that of the wonderful group of people around him, simply had to be told.

Not being too sure what I had jumped into doing, I began recording interviews less than twenty-four hours after he won the Plate. It was when I sent that first note to FriesenPress in January 2021, indicating I wanted to self publish, that I realized, I am really writing my first book.

I had some amazing help. Neil A. Campbell, who got me my first handicapping gig in the *Globe & Mail* all those years ago, offered advice and words from start to finish. Neil, I owe you a ham sandwich. Susan Stafford-Pooley, thank you for reading through all those early chapters. I promise to give you a winner one day!

Thank you Lisa J. for your guidance on everything bookish over the years and for being a friend; Vicki Pappas, who is responsible for getting me my first racetrack job and starting this whole, amazing career thing, and her hubby Bill Diamant for keeping me (somewhat) sane during the tough winter months of 2021, allowing me to enjoy watching racing with both of you every weekend.

Thank you to Jim Lawson for your kind words and always being available and to Jamie Dykstra and Jessica Buckley for your help at the track.

To Larry Cordes, thank you so much for your help in getting this book off the ground and for all the times I called you and asked you the same questions over again. Larry would like to dedicate the Mighty Heart story to the late Gerry Aschinger and his wife Dana for their role in bringing Mighty Heart into the world. Thank you to the entire 'Mighty' family: Angela, Jennifer, Darin, Megan, Siobhan Brown and Josie Carroll for telling your stories with passion.

The Mighty Heart story is brought to life by the many gorgeous images and candid snapshots so very generously donated to me by some wonderful people. There are so many great people who enjoy coming out to the racetrack and take gobs of images simply just to post them on social media, purely for the love of the sport. Thank you John Watkins, Mr. Will Wong, Laurie Langley, Santino DiPaola, Brittany Troxtell, Jeff Bowen, Terence and Cindy Dulay, Adrienne Shaw, Lousie Reinegal and Dave Landry.

Thank you Michael Burns, Jr., Churchill Downs and the Canadian Horse Racing Hall of Fame for photos and Ed Walton for that cool Picov Downs program page featuring Evelyn Cordes' College Fund and Hayley Badner from The Loose Girth for the photo of the Mighty Heart cookies.

Thank you to Debbie Anderson and Leanne Janzen and the editors and layout folks at FriesenPress, a very exciting experience!

I had some awesome cheer-leading friends. Laurel Miller-Junk offered to read through one of the last versions of the book and her insight and corrections were invaluable. Laurel is part of our beloved 'book club' (we do discuss a book we have read but also enjoy a few adult beverages) that has been so therapeutic for me; thank you Jen Bell and Cathy Geddes. And thank you Renée Kierans and Lisa Hocking for always lending an ear.

My amazing family provided me with pep talks when I wasn't sure if I could write a book, never mind get through a pandemic. I sure needed them. In particular my 'mole sista', Andrea Strohak Morrison, who absolutely is always there for me. I have the greatest brother in the world, Andrew, who selflessly will drop everything to help me. Their sons Connor and Graham are the most wonderful nephews a gal could have.

Thank you Maureen Mitchell-Morrison for all your help and words of encouragement.

And lots of love to Eric and his son Damien for cheering me on and to Jake, for not allowing me to sit longer than a few hours at a time before I had to take you for a walk.

And of course, thank you to Mighty Heart. ♥ I hope you know how many people you touched.

Jennifer Morrison, September 24, 2020

SOURCES

"A Short History About Penetanguishene." Accessed 10 February 2021. https://www.penetanguishene.ca/en/discover/history.asp

Bayfield, John. "Penetanguishene. 12 October 2012. Accessed 01 February 2021. https://www.thecanadianencyclopedia.ca/en/article/penetanguishene

Cauz, Louis E. & Beverly Smith. The Plate: 150 Years of Royal Tradition from Don Juan to Eye of the Leopard. Toronto: ECW Press. 2009.

"Equix Cardio Capacity Scores." Accessed 04 February 2021. http://www.equixbio.com/thoroughbred-cardio-scores.php

Flaherty, Dave. "The legacy of Windfields Farm and Northern Dancer." 8 October 2019. https://oshawaexpress.ca/the-legacy-of-windfields-farm-and-northern-dancer/

Fraser, Jeremy. "Groves Point native overcomes epilepsy to serve as groom for Queen's Plate-winner Mighty Heart." 16 September, 2020. https://www.thechronicleherald.ca/sports/regional-sports/video-groves-point-native-overcomes-epilepsy-to-serve-as-groom-for-queens-plate-winner-mighty-heart-497951/

"Grand National Ultimate History." Accessed 30 March 2021. https://www.grandnationalultimatehistory.com/races-1911.html

Jones, Janet L., PHD."How Horses See the World." 16 February 2016. https://equusmagazine.com/riding/visual-discrepancies-31223

Lefko, Perry. "Josie Carroll is a good horse trainer not a good woman horse trainer." 27 June 2019. https://www.thoroughbreddailynews.com/josie-carroll-is-a-good-horse-trainer-not-a-good-woman-horse-trainer/

Lennox, Muriel. E.P. Taylor: A Horseman and His Horses. Toronto: Burns & MacEachern. 1976.

Milton, Steve. "Where did the inspirational Mighty Heart story start? In Hamilton." 29 October 2020. https://www.thespec.com/sports/hamilton-region/opinion/2020/10/29/where-did-the-inspirational-mighty-heart-story-start-in-hamilton.html

APPENDICES:
More on Mighty Heart

Bay colt, born April 5, 2017

Owner and breeder: Lawrence Cordes, Uxbridge, Ontario

Trainer: Josie Carroll, from Mississauga, Ontario

Foaled at: Curraghmore Farm, Waterdown, Ontario

Race Record (through November 15, 2021)

Won: Queen's Plate, Prince of Wales Stakes, Autumn Stakes (Grade 2), Dominion Day Stakes (Grade 3), Blame Stakes

Year	Starts	1st	2nd	3rd	Earnings
2021	7	3	2	1	$399,315
2020	8	3	0	1	$922,870
Lifetime	15	6	2	2	$1,322,185

*Canadian earnings

Pedigree of Mighty Heart, bay colt, April 5, 2017

			Mr. Prospector
		Forty Niner	File
	Distorted Humor		Danzig
Sire		Danzig's Beauty	Sweetest Chant
Dramedy			Seattle Slew
		A.P. Indy	Weekend Surprise
	She's a Winner		Mr. Prospector
		Get Lucky	Dance Number
			Storm Bird
		Storm Cat	Terlingua
	City Place		Glitterman
Dam		Glitter Woman	Carois Folly
Emma's Bullseye			Afleet
		Northern Afleet	Nuryette
	Fleeting April		Sunny Clime
		April's Luci	April Moment (family 42)

Josie Carroll with Mighty Heart
in the summer of 2021. Photo by Jeff Bowen.

Links to Learn More About Horse Racing

Alcohol and Gaming Corporation Ontario – www.agco.on.ca

Canadian Thoroughbred – www.canadianthoroughbred.com

Canadian Thoroughbred Horse Society (Ontario) – www.cthsont.com

Horsemen's Benevolent and Protective Association (Ontario)
www.hbpa.on.ca

Jockey Club of Canada – www.jockeyclubcanada.com

LongRun Thoroughbred Retirement Society
www.longrunretirement.com

Ontario Racing – www.ontarioracing.com

Woodbine Entertainment – www.woodbine.com

CPSIA information can be obtained
at www.ICGtesting.com
Printed in the USA
LVHW072204140323
741574LV00018B/85/J

9 781039 128385